The International
Urban Crisis

The International Urban Crisis

Thomas L. Blair

ⓦ HILL AND WANG   New York
A division of Farrar, Straus and Giroux

1 2 3 4 5 6 7 8 9 10

Library of Congress Cataloging in Publication Data

Blair, Thomas Lucien Vincent.
    The international urban crisis.
    Bibliography: p.
    1. Cities and towns.   2. Cities and towns—Planning—1945–
        I. Title.
HT151.B55   301.36   73-75186
ISBN: 0-8090-9536-X   *strand /695/344/ 1/25/75*

Acknowledgements

Acknowledgement is made to the following for the use of previously published material, in addition to that credited in the text:

Tables 1 and 2 – *United Nations Statistical Yearbook* (copyright © United Nations 1968). Reproduced by permission.

Table 3 – *United Nations Statistical Yearbook* (copyright © United Nations 1969). Reproduced by permission.

Table 4 – *The Common Market and the Common Man* (June 1972), published by the European Communities.

Table 5 – *Social Statistics Yearbook 1970* of the Statistical Office of the European Communities.

Table 6 – *Battle for the Environment* by Tony Aldous (Fontana).

Map 3 – *The Challenge of Megalopolis* by Wolf Von Eckhardt, based on the original study by Jean Gottmann, copyright © The Twentieth Century Fund Inc. 1964. All rights reserved.

Contents

Chapter 1   *Urban Explosion*   15

  Dynamic Forces on a Global Scale   15
  World Urban Growth   23
  Urbanizing Societies   25
  The Challenge of Megalopolis   38

Chapter 2   *Slums and Suburbs*   45

  What Is a Slum?   45
  Slums Grow   48
  Suburbs Scatter   51
  Slums in the Suburbs   58
  Taming Decay and Sprawl   61

Chapter 3   *Movement and Congestion*   66

  Urban Transport in Crisis   67
  The American Case   78
  The 'Anti-City'   91

Chapter 4   *Pollution and the Environment*   96

  Urban Pollution   96
  Pollution Spreads   104
  What Is Being Done?   108
  Cities Are out of Phase   114

Chapter 5   *Alienation, Conflict, and Violence*   117

  City Problems in Perspective   117
  Alienation   120
  Poverty and Inequality   121
  Blocked Opportunity   124
  Black Ghetto Revolt   130

Violence-prone Cities   134
Dialectics of Disorder   138

Chapter 6 *Search for Solutions*   141

New Movement in the City   141
New Towns, New Frontiers?   145
Towards Metropolitan–Regional Management   151
Reforming Government Structures   154
Planning Urban Futures   157
People and Planning   161

Bibliography   167

Index   173

Tables and Maps

Chapter 1 – Urban Explosion

Table 1 Distribution of the Estimated World Population
(Mid-1967) and Annual Rates of Increase   16
Table 2 The Fifteen Countries with the Largest Populations 18
Table 3 The Multi-million Cities: Twenty-six Urban
Agglomerations   19
Table 4 Foreign Workers in the European Community   20

Map 1 The Community's Regions   22
Map 2 The Golden Triangle   39
Map 3 The 'Bos-Wash', U.S.A. East Coast Megalopolis   41
Map 4 Great Lakes Megalopolis   42
Map 5 Urban Detroit Area   43

Chapter 2 – Slums and Suburbs

Table 5 Stock of Dwellings in the European Economic
Community   49

Chapter 3 – Movement and Congestion

Table 6 Increase in Number of Motor Vehicles in Britain   71
Table 7 Europe's Motorways   77
Table 8 Automobile Ownership by Income Group,
U.S.A., 1966   85

Note: The term 'billion' as used throughout this text represents the equivalent of 1,000 million.

Preface

The major ills of our time are brutally apparent in the giant centres of population, finance, trade, and culture – the multi-million cities like New York, London, Tokyo, Paris, and Moscow. Everywhere the pattern is depressingly similar: unplanned growth, inner-city decay and suburban sprawl, twice-daily traffic jams on roads and underground transit systems, misused public funds, unrelieved poverty, slums still uncleared and growing larger, power and water shortages, and polluted environments. The richer the resources, the worse the mess.

What has gone wrong? Why does homelessness and squalor grow on a gigantic scale? Why are traffic and transport facilities strained to breaking point and no longer able to meet the travelling needs of urban dwellers? What are the forces of metropolitan growth that push whole communities into oblivion and kill the last vestiges of small-scale neighbourhood living? Why are urban planners, politicians, and administrators so insensitive to the needs of people and, more frighteningly, unable to cope with the mounting crisis in cities?

This book analyses these questions by examining the most urgent problems facing urban man in an age of chaotic growth, predatory technology, and exploitative economic development. Specific examples are drawn from the great world metropolitan centres to indicate the limitations of cities and the human problems they create. My conclusions are that we do not know enough about the main trends shaping our lives in a predominantly urbanized world. We do not know what the consequences will be for human life, nor the full scope of the irreversible damage being done by present-day practices. The urban crisis is universal – it is a crisis of human settlements and of the discordant siren's song of 'progress' which draws them ever closer to disaster. If we are to halt the decline then new modes of public and private action must be initiated, and radical reforms introduced at all levels of life to achieve a more humane and socially just urban future.

THOMAS L. BLAIR

The International
Urban Crisis

1 Urban Explosion

Cities are where the action is: the new science-based automated industries, jobs, wages, consumer markets, political decision-making, and renascent arts and culture. They provide the setting in which capital, labour, and innovative genius produce the feats of modern technology that radically change our habits, ways of life, and the man-made environment. Today millions of people are seeking progress and material advancement in urban centres. Their massive entry into the city unleashes the awesome prospect of an urban explosion: a five-fold increase in numbers, heavy pressure on already overloaded urban facilities and dangerously polluted settlements, and the rapid deterioration of the urban environment and the human condition.

Dynamic Forces on a Global Scale

Three major forces are shaping the future of the cities of the world. The first is the unprecedented growth in world populations; the second is the massive movement of people from the land and their increasing concentration in cities; and the third is rapid economic development and technological change. If any of these get out of balance and control – and there are already signs that they have – the impact on man's urban habitat could be disastrous.

In the course of man's history, from the Stone Age to the present, the rate of population growth has increased a thousand-fold – from a mere 2 per cent per millennium to an awesome 2 per cent per annum. Given the same rate, there are grave forecasts for the future of this finite planet. Today's 3 billions could become a fantastic 50 billion population in 142 years. This rate of growth, says the demographer Philip Hauser in Ronald Freedman's book *Population: The Vital Revolution*, would in 237 years produce

15

enough people standing shoulder to shoulder to reach from the earth to the sun. On our crowded planet there would be one person per square foot of land surface, including mountains, deserts, and the Arctic waters, and in 1,566 years the population would weigh as much as the earth itself.

This great leap in population growth is a very recent factor in our lives – only three centuries old – and is accelerating rapidly, bursting into our awareness as 'the Population Explosion'. To grasp its implications one need only be able to count to 5 billion.

ONE: it took most of the millennia of man's habitation of this planet to produce 1 billion persons simultaneously alive. This was reached in 1850. TWO: to produce 2 billion population required an additional seventy-five years. This was achieved in 1925. THREE: to reach 3 billion required only an additional thirty-seven years. This was the total in 1962. FOUR: continuation of this trend would produce a fourth billion in about fifteen years, i.e. 1977, and ... BOOM! ... a fifth billion in less than an additional ten years.

Table 1

Distribution of the Estimated World Population (Mid-1967) and Annual Rates of Increase

Location		Population (in millions)	Annual rate of increase, 1960–67
World		3,420	1·9
Africa		328	2·4
America	North	220	1·4
	Latin	259	2·9
Asia	East	877	1·4
	South	1,030	2·5
Europe		452	0·9
Oceania		18	2·0
Soviet Union		236	1·4

Source: *United Nations Statistical Yearbook*, 1968.

This accelerated population growth is without historical precedent. Data gathered for the United Nations Statistical Yearbook at more than 250 observation posts around the world emphasize this. By mid-1968 the world's population had reached almost 3½ billion at an annual growth rate of 1·9 per cent. Every day 320,000 births cancelled out 140,000 deaths and produced an increase of 180,000 new world citizens to be nurtured and reared. If this rate continues, it is estimated, the world's population will double in thirty-nine years.

The cause of this acceleration is not, as many people might believe, increased fertility in human populations. Far from it. The cause lies in the unprecedented decline in mortality which, while fertility remains constant, produces larger rates of population growth. As a consequence, unlike any previous stage in man's history, fertility, or the birth rate, has become the principal dynamic variable in population change. It is now ominously clear that man in the 1970s may be confronted with a higher rate of population growth than has ever occurred before. And it will keep on growing in the foreseeable future at a rate of about 1 per cent per annum in the developed countries and 2·5 per cent in most of the Third World, i.e. the poorer nations of Africa, Asia, and Latin America.

Today 40 per cent of the world's population lives in urban areas and their numbers are growing at a faster rate, 3·5 per cent, than rural populations, 1 per cent. And this trend is greater in the Third World, 4·4 per cent, than in the more developed countries, 2·9 per cent.

If these trends continue, then by 1990 the situation will be as follows. In the developed regions, where the total population will be larger by three quarters, urban populations will have nearly trebled. Europe's total population will be one quarter larger and its urban population will have grown by two thirds. In the Third World the number of inhabitants of towns and cities will multiply by four in East Africa, by five in middle South Asia and in northern and southern Africa, by six in other parts of Asia, by seven in Latin America, and by more than nine times in tropical Africa.

Large cities continue to bear the brunt of this massive growth. There are now 1,645 cities in the world with populations of 100,000 or more. Big cities with at least 500,000 inhabitants rose from 158 in 1950 to 234 in 1960; and the number of huge multi-million cities increased from twenty to twenty-six. Tokyo and New York, with more than 11 millions in their central cities, suburbs, and densely settled adjoining areas, vie for the position of the world's largest urban agglomeration.

Table 2

The Fifteen Countries with the Largest Populations

Country	Population (in millions)
China (Mainland)	730*
India	524
Soviet Union	238
U.S.A.	201
Indonesia	113
Pakistan	110
Japan	101
Brazil	88
Nigeria	63*
Germany (Fed. Rep.)	58
United Kingdom	55
Italy	53*
France	50
Mexico	47
Philippines	36

*Estimated by the United Nations.

Source: *United Nations Demographic Yearbook*, 1968.

In the process, the major cities have grown into huge metropolitan regions and encompass a larger proportion of their national populations than ever before. According to recent statistics, 22·5 per cent of the population of the United Kingdom live in London; 16·8 per cent of all Frenchmen live in Paris; 15·7 per cent of all Belgians are in Brussels; 14·5 per cent of the Japanese are in the Tokyo–Yokohama metropolitan area; 19·3 per cent of the Germans are in the Rhine–Ruhr complex of cities; and 33·1 per cent of the Dutch are in the seven-city Randstad area.

America's most productive and wealthy urban area, the New York–New Jersey metropolitan region, has about 14 million people, or 8·2 per cent of the American population; and as its population rises to the figure of 21 million by 1985 and 30 million by AD 2000 the region's proportion of the total national population is also expected to rise dramatically.

It seems as if the future for most countries in the world is one where most of the population will live in cities, and a large proportion of that number will be concentrated in the biggest, most congested metropolises.

Table 3

The Multi-million Cities:
Twenty-six Urban Agglomerations

Agglomeration	Population (in millions)
New York	14·2
Tokyo	13·5
London	8·2
Shanghai	7·5
Paris	7·1
Buenos Aires	6·8
Los Angeles	6·6
Moscow	6·2
Chicago	6·0
Calcutta	5·8
Osaka	5·2
Ruhrgebiet	5·0
Mexico City	4·8
Rio de Janeiro	4·7
São Paulo	4·4
Bombay	4·0
Philadelphia	3·7
Detroit	3·6
Peking	3·5
Leningrad	3·4
Cairo	3·3
Berlin	3·3
Djakarta	2·8
Tientsin	2·8
Boston	2·7
Hong Kong	2·6

Source: United Nations, *Report on The World Population Situation*, 1969 (based on 1960 figures).

The third factor in the urban revolution is rapid economic growth and development, and technological change. World economic growth continues to rise steeply each decade. The major growth sectors are industrial production, mining, manufacturing, energy production, transport vehicles, tourism, and international trade. World exports have reached an all-time record of $238,000 million. This pattern of growth is as typical of the Soviet Union and the socialist or centrally planned economies as it is of the North American, European, and capitalist market economies.

The hectic pace of economic activity is the hallmark of modern societies. Nations and powerful international companies are competing for the resources of economic development, technological innovation, and consumer markets. The products of

Table 4

Foreign Workers in the European Community (1970–71)

Country	Foreign workers	Proportion from community nations (mainly Italians)	Foreign workers as percentage of total working population
Belgium	208,000	117,000	5·5
France	1,200,000	280,000	5·8
Germany	2,241,000	530,000	8·3
Italy	39,000	12,000	0·2
Luxembourg	33,000	26,000	23·0
Netherlands	125,000	49,000	2·7

Source: *The Common Market and the Common Man*, p. 7. European Communities Press and Information, Brussels, published June 1972.

science and technology tumble from the workshops of the world: antibiotics, pain killers and prophylactics, synthetic fibres and bulk plastics, single-cell protein, computerized knowledge and communications, automated machines of war and peace, and large-scale development plans for hydro-electric power, irrigation, reservoirs, and dams. New modes of production, life, and labour are introduced which have many uncontrolled, unforeseen, and unplanned effects on human behaviour and traditional social institutions.

Cities are the focal points of change and opportunity. And as mobile workers and their families move towards cities, declining areas become increasingly depopulated and job centres correspondingly congested. Pressures mount on outmoded and inadequate urban housing and public services. And the major question facing societies in transition is how to accommodate the increasing numbers of people entering urban-based economies, i.e. economies where the major portion of the labour force must earn its living in congested urban areas.

Migration from rural and stagnant regions to thriving urban job centres in developing regions is the single most important stimulus for urban growth. Migrant workers and their families are on the move all over the world as part of a massive international trade in manpower. They are driven to move by hunger, land shortages, and unemployment, and drawn to cities by the promise of a tomorrow filled with remunerative employment, better housing and education, and higher living standards.

In Europe, 5 million migrant workers are the stokers of the overheated economies of the Common Market nations. They take jobs that nationals refuse because of low wages and bad working conditions in building and construction, public services, textiles and clothing, metallurgy and heavy engineering, mining, catering, and domestic service. And thereby they make a major contribution to the development of the world's fastest-growing production and marketing centre.

Migrants move from depressed areas, regional pockets of poverty, and forgotten rural backlands. Today's urban newcomers in Europe might be a farm labourer from Brittany who got fed up with working seventy hours a week and opted for a forty-hour factory job; a Flemish farmer's daughter now working as a semi-skilled apprentice in a modern American-owned chemical plant near Antwerp; or a strapping, olive-skinned Italian youth from the poverty-stricken Mezzogiorno region who left his family's hillside hovel to work in a Belgian coal-mine or on a building site in Munich or Milan. And in recent years more migrants have come from less-developed areas outside Western Europe. Germany recruits Spaniards, Greeks, Turks, Moroccans, Italians, Portuguese, Yugoslavs, Tunisians, and South Koreans. Britain has her Irishmen, West Indians, Indians, and Pakistanis, as well as Italians and Spaniards. France has Algerians and other North Africans, Antilleans, and West Africans along with Spaniards and Portuguese. Holland has her Turks, West Indians, Greeks, and Italians, along with Indonesian refugees. In Belgium the migrants are mainly Italians, Turks, and Greeks.

Map 1: The Community's Regions
Density of industrial and agricultural populations
The regional units shown are French and Italian planning regions, German Länder, and Belgian and Netherlands provinces.

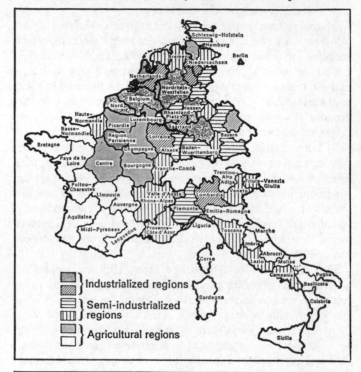

Type of Region	Criteria		Percentage of the EEC	
	Percentage of working population in agriculture	Density of population	By area	By population
Industrialized regions	Up to 10 10–20	Over 250/km² Over 200/km²	9 7	30 11
Semi-industrialized regions	Up to 15 Over 15	Over 150/km² Under 150/km²	9 21	12·5 19
Agricultural regions	20–30 30	Under 100/km² Under 100/km²	12 42	6 21·5

Source: *European Community* (Journal), December 1969, p.11.

Cities and job centres in the newly developing areas of the Third World are also focal points of migration. Today twelve of the twenty-four cities in the world with populations of over 500,000 are to be found in the Third World. And in the next forty years, as millions of people migrate to cities in the southern hemisphere of the globe, the increase in city dwellers alone will be double that of the world's total population growth in the last 6,000 years.

World Urban Growth

World urban growth has been systematically studied by a number of well-known investigators, for example, Charles Abrams, a United Nations housing consultant, Gideon Sjoberg, author of a provocative book, *The Preindustrial City*, about the origins and evolution of cities, and Professor Kingsley Davis, director of the International Population and Urban Research Agency of the University of California at Berkeley. Professor Davis, a demographer who has devoted a lifetime to the study of cities, has devised a system for comparing data on the proportion of people living in the large world cities. The unit of measurement is the 'Standard Metropolitan Area' used by the United States Bureau of the Census. It is defined as 'an urban unit containing at least 100,000 people in an area embracing a central city or cities, plus adjacent areas with an economic relationship with that city, and with 65 per cent or more of their economically active population engaged in non-agricultural activities'.

When Professor Davis correlated his results with historical data on city populations he discovered two interesting patterns. The proportion of the population living in cities of 100,000 or more accelerated and was higher in the one hundred years from 1850 to 1950 than from 1800 to 1850, but the rate of change between 1950 and 1960 was twice as high as that of the preceding century. At this rate, he concluded, by the end of the twentieth century, more than half the people in the world would be living in cities of 100,000 or more. 'Clearly,' he said, 'the world is not fully urbanized, but it soon may be.'

The shift of populations from rural to urban areas and the sustained growth of cities are major characteristics of advanced Western industrial societies. In Britain, the population of major urban areas is expanding more rapidly than anywhere else in the country. Already more than 80 per cent live in urban areas and 30 per cent alone live in cities of 100,000 persons or more. Between now and AD 2000 it is estimated that the national population may increase by 40 per cent, and a large proportion of this expansion will take place in cities.

More than 70 per cent of the American population are urban dwellers, living in large dense agglomerations that involve an unprecedented intensity of human contact and diversity. According to the 1960 census nearly 52 million people, or about a quarter of the national population, lived in sixteen major urban areas on a total land area less than the size of a small county in Arizona. And 96 million people – just over half the nation's 180 million population – were concentrated in 213 urban areas that occupied less than 1 per cent of the total national land area.

The Soviet Union is moving in the same direction, mainly because of rural to urban migration. In 1939 32 per cent of the Russian people, some 60 million, were classified as urban. By 1959 it was 48 per cent or 99·8 million. During the same period the population of the biggest cities, those with over 100,000, grew dramatically from 23·1 to 33·5 million in the western regions and from 5·7 million to 14·8 million in the eastern regions.

The booming cities of Asia today were the huge trading entrepôts of the colonial era: Delhi, Bombay, Calcutta, Singapore, Hong Kong, Manilla, and Djakarta. Hong Kong, a rapidly industrializing British colony, provides a special example of the rapid growth of Asian cities. The colony's population multiplied six times since 1945; the urban area, which includes Kowloon and New Kowloon, has a density of more than 200,000 per square mile. (By contrast, Delhi, usually considered an extreme example of population growth, has an average density of 136,000 per square mile.)

Major population growth has taken place in the metropolises of Latin America: Buenos Aires, São Paulo, Rio de Janeiro, Mexico City, Santiago, and Lima. Caracas quintupled in the twenty years 1945–65, and Bogotá trebled its population. Argentina, the most urbanized Latin American nation, already has most of its 22 million people living in towns and cities. One third of the population cluster in Greater Buenos Aires, the economic heart of the nation and one of the largest metropolitan areas in the world.

In Africa cities with more than 100,000 inhabitants have grown at a rate of 9 per cent per annum, or double the rate of the continent's entire population. By 1960 8 per cent of all the people in Africa lived in cities of 100,000 or more and 13 per cent lived in places of 20,000 or more. Though Africa is the least urbanized major world region, its urban growth rate is among the highest in the world and more than double the world average. Today there are 30 million urban-dwelling Africans in the larger cities alone and their numbers are increasing rapidly because of in-migration at a rate of 3 million a year.

Migration, coupled with natural increases, has led to a phenomenal growth in the population of Chinese cities. China's 77 million urban population in 1953 exceeded that of every country in the world except America and the Soviet Union, and has probably risen considerably to 100 million in recent years. Between 1949 and 1956 alone some 20 million Chinese migrated from rural to urban areas. It was a massive movement that Gerald Breese in his book *Urbanization in Newly Developing Countries* calls one of history's largest population shifts in so short a time. The urban population lived in 164 'municipalities' (i.e. large and medium-sized cities) and 5,404 towns, and represented about 13 per cent of the then 580 million mainland Chinese. China's three northeast provinces are the most highly urbanized, particularly Hopeh, which includes Peking and Tientsin, and Kiangsu, which includes Shanghai. In addition, cities in the western provinces underwent an amazing growth due to migration from the rural periphery and as far as the industrial centres of Manchuria and East China.

Urbanizing Societies

The world trend is clearly towards urbanized societies in which a majority of the people live in towns and cities. Such societies are a new and fundamental step in man's social evolution. They grow out of dramatic economic and technological changes and the switch from a spread-out national settlement pattern to concentration in urban centres. Before 1850 no society was predominantly urbanized. By 1900 only one, Britain, was. Now all industrial nations are highly urbanized and in the world as a whole urbanization is accelerating.

Seen from a historical perspective, urbanized societies are the latest stage in the evolution of cities and city-based cultures. Cities are a form of human organization devised over thousands of years as a means of organizing production, communication, and social relations within a densely settled area. Their major role is to combine in a fixed place the special functions – economic, political, technical, and cultural – which are needed in the service of the wider society of which they are a part. Three stages stand out as of paramount importance. One is the development of city-based ancient civilizations out of small folk societies through the introduction of irrigation, metalworking and the production of economic surpluses. Another is the conquest of the environment and the organization and monopoly of capital, time, and labour which marked the creation of the nineteenth-century industrial city. And thirdly, the internationalization of finance and trade which accompanied the rise of the modern metropolis.

Sedentary folk societies of 5,500 years ago are the remotest antecedents of today's modern cities. They were small, homogeneous, and self-sufficient groups of kith and kin who established village settlements and staked a claim upon the land around them as their own. Their lives were centred on wresting food and shelter from a hostile environment. In time they formed stable and productive communities. Through the application of animate sources of energy and rudimentary technology, such as irrigation, metalworking, the animal-drawn plough, and the wheeled cart, they raised food production above the level of subsistence and freed manpower to produce goods for barter and trade.

Crossroad villages and trading centres grew and dominated their rural sources of food, wood, and water. Powerful leaders accumulated capital through tribute and taxes, organized artisanal production for trade, and created thriving city-states and empires. These changes signalled the rise of the first great cities and the transformation of folk societies into the pre-industrial urban-based civilizations of antiquity.

The world's first cities began about 3500 BC in the fertile Tigris–Euphrates valley of what is now Iraq, and in the Indus valley of Pakistan at Mohenjo-Daro and Harappa. Cities also appeared in the Yellow River valley in China and the Nile valley in Egypt. Despite their differences, these cities shared many common features: cereal farming, bronze-working, artisans, written records, and dependence on limited sources of power, whether the wind and water, or the shoulders of men and the backs of animals.

In time, cities flourished along the Mediterranean Sea, and in Africa and the New World. Miletus, Athens, Alexandria, Carthage, and Syracuse along the Mediterranean coast had populations varying from 30,000 to 100,000. Rome under Augustus had more than 300,000 permanent residents. In the Byzantine and Arab worlds there were large settlements of 200,000 to 300,000 people at Byzantium, Antioch, Damascus, Cairo, and Baghdad, capital of the Caliphate empire. Córdoba and Seville in Moorish Spain each had between 50,000 and 90,000 inhabitants.

Tropical Africa had its city-based civilizations of Oyo and Benin, Kanem and Mali in the west, Kongo and Monomotapa to the south; and its riverheads and coastlines sheltered large centres for regional and transoceanic trade. In the New World, the Maya, Zapotec, and Aztec civilizations of Meso-America built stable settlements of 3,000 to 8,500 dwellings and ceremonial structures at Tikal, Guatemala, and Dzibilchaltún, Yucatan, and Teotihuacán near present-day Mexico City had a population of 100,000 in the first millennium AD.

Most of these cities were comparatively small in size by contemporary standards, and together probably contained no more than 2 per cent of the world's total population. Urban growth was restricted by the limited availability of food resources to feed city dwellers. Yet populations did grow, and cities absorbed more land. They did so because skills and techniques were developed for converting human and natural resources into economic goods and services. As a consequence they became the workshops and seed-beds of economic growth in what sociologists call 'pre-industrial societies'; i.e. large states and empires whose economies developed with increased production of commodities for trade. The most powerful cities were rapacious centres of government and commerce that fed upon the hinterlands. Their power lay in military might, political regimentation, and imperialist control. Their affluence was based on the effective organization of slavery, gang labour, and the estate plantation system to exploit the countryside.

For example, in Athens and Rome, the first great European urban-based pre-industrial civilizations, when the rapid growth of city populations put heavy pressure on the productive capacity of the land, more distant areas were plundered. Hills, mountains, and forests were laid bare. Outlying provinces in southern Europe and North Africa were ruthlessly exploited, exhausted, and abandoned one by one to feed a growing proletariat and enrich the prosperous with loot. The huge granaries of Rome, Latium,

27

Campania, Sardinia, Sicily, Spain, and northern Africa were all successively reduced to barren wastes, swamplands, and deserts, and few of them have ever recovered from the devastating effects of that era.

Pre-industrial societies and their cities highlighted the appearance of two new phenomena, urbanization and urbanism. The former required that more people were pushed off the land and pulled into larger settlements; the latter the emergence of a new culture of cities. Its basic components were social heterogeneity and the declining importance of family and kinship ties, a mode of production increasingly dependent on a high degree of specialization of labour, non-agricultural occupations, technological innovation and change, and a centralized city-based governmental structure.

It was in pre-industrial societies that cities gained their dualistic identification as both creatures and creators of new social processes. They were, on the one hand, a necessary and integral part of a wider functioning entity – an empire, an organized social order, a civilization. And at the same time, the city helped shape great civilizations and influenced many differing cultures with which it came into contact. For example, Rome diffused an urban culture as far afield as France, Britain, the Low Countries, Germany west of the Rhine, and central and eastern Europe.

The fall of Rome heralded the end of the pre-industrial city as far as Europe was concerned. Cities declined in size between AD 450 and AD 950. Here and there a new town occasionally arose around a church, a river crossing, or an old Roman camp. The town walls were extended if populations grew, but when epidemics struck, urban dwellers abandoned the city for the countryside. From the Middle Ages to the seventeenth century, European city growth was severely limited by disease and the continuance of an agrarian tradition. Most centres were no more than hamlets or small towns. Towards the end of the Renaissance, Venice and Rome doubled their populations; London and Paris had hundreds of thousands of residents and were emerging as the giants of Europe. They were important as administrative, commercial, and cultural centres, but still only a small proportion of the whole population lived in them.

New conditions for change were created in the seventeenth and eighteenth centuries. A turning point in the history of cities was at hand. The nefarious slave trade and slave labour harnessed to the colonial production of agricultural and mineral resources brought riches to Europe. Trade expanded, capital was accumulated, effective communications systems and transport lines were established. There was a marked growth of urban-centred handicraft and food-manufacturing industries. At the same time millions of people in Europe were poised to make the move to cities. Medical and dietary advances had cut the mortality rate, and increased productivity per farm worker had reduced rural manpower requirements. As a result rural areas were plagued with overpopulation and unemployment. Jobless and landless peasants were pushed off the land and pulled towards the urban market-place. And with their entry into urban employment centres the industrial city arose as the pre-eminent symbol of the Industrial Revolution. It was the central place, *par excellence*, where men, machines, and capital were co-ordinated to produce goods for world markets.

England, the first urbanized and industrialized nation, is the classic example of this process. Between 1811 and 1891 the total population of England's large cities (100,000 inhabitants or more) increased from 1·2 million to more than 9·2 million. And in terms of the aggregate urban population, in 1891 44 per cent resided in London and twenty-three other large cities. London, a mud-flat on the banks of the Thames River when Caesar arrived, grew from 800 thousand to more than 4 million between 1801 and 1891 – an increase of almost 400 per cent – and, with an additional 1·6 million people in the surrounding settlements, became the world's largest city. This colossal concentration of working people plus factories and financial institutions linked with transoceanic trade made England and its capital the major commercial entrepôt of the world.

The pattern in other Western industrializing nations was similar: mass migration to cities, the doubling and trebling of city populations, and a resultant increase in the proportion of people living in cities. By the latter decades of the nineteenth century cities of 10,000 or more people contained 26 per cent of the French population and over 15 per cent of the populations of Germany, Austria, and Sweden. Almost all the mass movement was to the largest cities, notably Paris, Stockholm, Vienna, and Budapest. Cities with 100,000 or more people increased from 22 in 1800 to 120 in 1895. In the same period their proportion of

29

the total European population advanced from less than 3 per cent to 10 per cent.

The rise of the nineteenth-century industrial city brought wealth and power to some, a façade of urbanity to others, but it was achieved at tremendous social cost: chronic economic depressions, spoil heaps, child labour, cholera epidemics, and oppressive working and living conditions. Many gallant men and women sought gradual reform through better housing, public health measures, and social legislation. Others under the banner of a new ideology, socialism, sought a more radical and fundamental change in the economic system which, by the intolerable conditions it created and the abuses it countenanced, alienated, dehumanized, and cast in ever-increasing numbers the spent hulks of urban humanity on to the slag heaps of society. Industrial workers responded with every weapon at their command: individual acts of crime, sabotage, and the destruction of machines and factories, trade unionism, strikes, class solidarity, and class consciousness. It seemed that the crisis of capitalism was at hand, and that if it did not topple of its own accord it would be overthrown by urban insurrection. But, though regimes were changed, capitalism surged forward to a new phase of major expansion.

The metropolis – a huge multi-million population centre of trade, finance, culture, and world power – is the dominant form of the twentieth century. It is the workshop, showplace, and boardroom of expanding urban societies. In it machine technology, economic rationalism, and political strategy are mobilized to achieve world power, profitable mass consumer markets, and spheres of influence.

The metropolis combines the function of central leadership and production of the main bulk of material goods and services. Its influence consolidates huge areas up to 100 miles outside the central city into vast metropolitan regions. Three definitive types have been identified: the monocentric region centred on a single major central area, like London or Paris; the bicentric or twin-headed region such as the Tokyo–Yokohama or the New York–Northeastern New Jersey complex; and the huge polycentric region composed of several contiguous metropolitan regions, e.g. the coal-mining-based cities of the Rhine–Ruhr region of Germany and the Dutch Randstad.

Great metropolises – like London, Paris, Moscow, Tokyo, the Randstad, and Rhine–Ruhr – exhibit the major problems of the urban explosion. They are dynamic, growing tentacular world cities, but they are also cities in trouble.

London

London has been the largest city in Britain since Roman times. It emerged from the cities of London, the financial and trade centre; Westminster, the seat of administration and government; and the development later of the West End as a residential and social centre. London's growth since the Industrial Revolution has been remarkable. Whereas in 1831 the compact urban area covered eighteen square miles and housed 1·65 million people, 125 years later the Greater London conurbation covered 722 square miles and had 8·2 million people.

Three concentric zones of activity ring the central heart of the city straddling the Thames: an inner zone of mixed industrial and residential land uses; the interwar middle-class suburbs; the green belt and the outer ring of towns surrounded by a maze of speculator-built estates. The London metropolitan area, which includes the conurbation and outer ring, contains 3,000 square miles and 11 million people, and is the biggest metropolitan area in Europe. After the New York–Northeastern New Jersey and Tokyo–Yokohama bicentric regions, it is the largest in the world.

London has occupied a place of world importance for ten centuries. It is the city of Regency squares and royal parks, Westminster, St Paul's, the Tower of London, Buckingham Palace, and great museums. Chaucer, Shakespeare, and Shaw, the Romans and Normans, the Tudors and Stuarts, Christopher Wren and Prince Albert have all left their mark upon it. But London today is also the city of foul smells and noises, ugliness and litter, homelessness and poverty, confusion and congestion. The pleasant aspects so dear to the hearts of bourgeois romanticists are gone, or rapidly dwindling. Office development, hotel construction, and the tourist trade are booming. 'Swinging London' throbs, shakes, and rattles to a cacophony of pneumatic drills, pile-drivers, and lorries grinding ready-made concrete. Underground trains shake buildings; a plane a minute descends over London to Heathrow Airport, leaving a trail of ear-splitting noise; fire engines, police cars, and ambulances flash and wail their way through traffic.

The central core of the city is the focus of activity. Every day 6 million journeys are made by bus or on the Underground. Two million trips are taken into the central area alone by public transport. Only a few hundred thousand people live in that area but more than $1\frac{1}{2}$ million people work there. They comprise about a quarter of all the employed persons in the London region, and half of them are office employees.

New office development, the single most important employment growth factor, has led to more traffic congestion and more long journeys to work. Commuter rail fares are high, trains are overcrowded, congestion occurs at transfer points with public transport, service is deteriorating, and fares are rising because of the uneconomic necessity to carry heavy loads of commuters at peak hours. In the central city the inadequate street systems plus increasing volumes of pedestrian and vehicular traffic choke the major arteries. And in the background is the ever-present spectre of obsolescent housing and the need to raise the standards of amenities in zones of housing stress.

Paris

Growth and change has been so rapid in Paris that no one knows any longer what Paris really is or where it ends. Basically it encompasses a range of great diversity from the hustle and bustle of the great boulevards and the East End tenements to the open fields of Brie and Beauce, or the great forests of Fontainebleau to the south and Chantilly to the north – depending on your definition.

Today there are at least three entities called Paris: the historic city, the agglomeration, and the region. La Ville de Paris is the historic city created by the Romans. It has twenty-six arrondissements, or administrative units, ten of which roughly define the built-up Paris of 1860. It forms an oval containing 3 million persons on 105 square kilometres, bounded by the great rail termini. In it are the new well-paid jobs in finance, luxury shops, scientific research institutes, university professions, management, clerical, and skilled trades. The peripheral ten arrondissements contain the poor, and the large and small commercial and industrial enterprises. The outer suburbs of the Seine–Banlieue have high population densities, heavy industry, and great industrial areas like Boulogne–Billancourt.

Together the Ville de Paris and the outer suburbs comprise the Paris agglomeration, totalling some 7·3 million people within 463 square miles. A larger unit still, as defined by planners, is the Paris Region, which radiates some forty to sixty miles from Notre Dame Cathedral and covers 5,000 square miles. It is equivalent to 2·4 per cent of the land area of France, and has 8·5 million people – almost 20 per cent of the total French population. The region's population growth rate has been phenomenal – twice that of the nation itself. And this has been due to an unexpected rise in births, calculated as 40 per cent of the total increase, as well as immigration, which has accounted for 60 per cent of the increase in recent decades.

Congestions of people, jobs, and traffic are major problems. Suburban-dwelling workers face long daily journeys to work. The transport, road, and traffic management situation is chaotic. The entire stock of social capital – housing, water and sewerage facilities, schools and recreational services – needs rebuilding. And there is a disturbing and growing distinction between the modernity of the centre and the boring uniformity of the residential suburbs. In Paris, it seems, all the best things are concentrated in the central area, and all the rest is *le désert français*.

Moscow

Moscow is the premier city of the Union of Soviet Socialist Republics and world city of the European Communist nations. It has a population of some 6·5 million people and is the hub of a great urban complex which totals about 9 million people. It is the greatest urban complex of continental Europe, after the Rhine–Ruhr region, and the biggest metropolitan region based on a single city.

In a country where more than half the population lives in urban areas, Moscow is the dominant transport, cultural, and industrial centre. Eleven main rail lines and three major airports – Vnukovo, Sheremetyevo, and Domodedovo – are located there. It is the centre of culture and entertainment, e.g. the Bolshoi Ballet and the Moscow Arts Theatre, mass media, tourism, and pilgrimages to the tombs of Lenin and other Soviet heroes. Moscow University, the Academy of Sciences, the Lenin Library and Museum, and several hundred research institutes are centres of the Soviet knowledge industry. Moscow's growing engineering and consumer goods industries account for over 20 per cent of the national industrial output. All these factors make Moscow and its citizens major contributors to modern Soviet technological achievements – giant aeroplanes, sputniks, and moonwalkers.

Moscow can be defined in terms of four geographical areas. At the core is a central area of typical European-style buildings surrounded by a ring boulevard – the Sadovoye Ring – lined with commercial and residential blocks. Beyond this range are the suburban areas up to the new belt motorway which encircles the city at a radius of about eleven miles from the centre. Outside there is a green belt, some six miles wide, and, beyond, the satellite towns. Some of these are of recent origin, but most are pre-revolutionary towns which expanded with the growth of engineering industries after 1917.

Housing problems inherited from tsarist times, described so vividly in Maxim Gorki's *The Lower Depths*, and aggravated by the devastations of the Second World War, have been made more difficult by the influx of migrants who account for three fifths of the city's population increase. In addition there are grave problems relating to the location of industry and the resolution of traffic management problems. Finding a new ideology of planning to chart the way forward will present many difficulties to Marxist dialecticians. The manifesto of the First Congress of Soviet Architects in 1937 called for socialist realism, i.e. the combination of 'ideological content and truthfulness of artistic expression'. But this view requires re-analysis in the light of the new market-oriented productive and social relations in modern Soviet society.

Tokyo

Tokyo is a rich and powerful city: the largest in the world in terms of population and the second largest in area. Its national position is no less formidable. Tokyo is three times the size of Osaka, the second largest Japanese city, and over six times that of Kyoto. Sixty per cent of the head offices of the country's industrial and commercial enterprises are located in Tokyo, along with 28 per cent of the universities and almost half of all university students. In fact, Tokyo is the heart of Japan, containing in its central area the Imperial Palace, the Kasumigaseki district with its government offices, the Marunouchi district centre of business and politics, and the Ginza Street shopping district, well known for its expensive shops, night-time gaiety, and multi-coloured vari-form neon lights.

Yet Tokyo is a city of great paradoxes. Its factories produce the most sophisticated technological products – television, transistors, cameras, and cars – but its citizens have relatively low standards of living, and the poverty in the outlying provincial regions is appalling. Fantastic advances have been made in mass transport technology but planners cannot solve traffic jams and congestion caused by 3 million people criss-crossing the city each day. The new Tokaido Line Express can traverse the 300 miles to Osaka in three hours, while homeward-bound suburbanites are still fuming in a long queue of cars making the weekend exodus from the city.

Tokyo is the world's fastest-growing metropolitan region. Migrants from low-income rural areas account for 70 per cent of the population growth of 200,000 per year. The focal points are the booming inner business districts and the northern and southern suburban factory areas where incomes are twice the national figure and three times that of poor agricultural communities.

Tokyo grew from modest feudal beginnings in 1456 around the Edo fortress to 1·4 million in 1785. Its population was at that time larger than London's 900,000, though not as important in the world economy. But change was made fairly rapidly. Under the Tokugawa regime a consumer-goods industry developed to cater for the needs and whims of nobles and their large numbers of retainers, the samurai. Western innovations in communications and transport were introduced under the Meiji rule. When the Emperor Meiji came to power in 1868, says Ki Kimura, a historian and novelist, 'it was like the bursting of a dam behind which had accumulated the energies and forces of centuries. Japan set out to achieve in only a few decades what had taken centuries to develop in the West: the creation of a modern nation, with modern industries and political institutions and a modern pattern of society.'

By 1912 the city had spread westward on to high land away from the Bay; and industry spread south along the Bay coast towards the old and rapidly expanding port city of Yokohama. Today the city's large plants, heavy industries, refineries, and cement works, and a host of smaller suppliers of materials, components, and specialized services make up one of the most amazing workshops in the world.

At the centre of the metropolitan region is the old city with its twenty-three wards and suburbs administered by the Tokyo Metropolitan Government. Its 1960 population was 9,683,802, and by 1964 it had become the first city authority in the world with over 10 million people. With the adjacent port city of Yokohama, Tokyo forms a bicentric metropolitan region stretching some thirty miles from the centre along major rail lines, and having a total population of 12·3 million people. And the planners' region, used for development planning, extends up to seventy-five miles and, with satellite towns and green belts, had a 25·4 million population in 1960.

Change at the centre is a result of new offices and shops, rising land prices and the competition for space, bomb damage during the Second World War and anti-earthquake legislation. Eighty per cent of the low-income people are in overcrowded housing lacking amenities. New private-sector housing consists of either low-quality, barrack-like flats with few amenities or luxury apartments at exorbitant rents. In 1960 a million people or 17 per cent of the Tokyo city proper had no piped water and 88·5 per cent had no sewerage. Tokyo has one of the largest commuter movements in the world – 1,100,000 daily suburban commuters and rush-hour crowds of up to 3 millions – yet public transport is inadequate and there is a tremendous strain on rail lines, underground, bus, and streetcar systems.

The Randstad

The Randstad in Holland, a polycentric ring of cities, is the fourth greatest metropolitan centre of Western Europe after London, Paris, and the Rhine–Ruhr region. Its diverse functions are located in separate urban complexes. Government headquarters are in The Hague (604,000 population). Port and wholesaling facilities and heavy industry are in Rotterdam (731,000 population). Finance, culture, retailing, diversified industries, and light manufacturing are in a cluster together in the capital city of Amsterdam (867,000 population). In addition, there are three cities with between 100,000 and 250,000 people each – Haarlem, Leiden, and Utrecht – and a number of smaller clusters of towns. In 1963 the total Randstad population stood at 4·27 million, and contained 36 per cent of the entire Netherlands population on 5 per cent of the land.

The Randstad's growth is associated with three important factors: rapid population growth due mainly to natural increase; the shift of workers from agriculture to manufacturing and service industries; and the growth of oil, petro-chemical, iron and steel industries. In addition, governmental employment has increased, particularly in education and in the civil-service sector located in The Hague.

The Randstad began to form as early as 1900. By 1950 the sprawling low-density suburbs coalesced and now are so close that they form a giant horseshoe, open to the southeast. The major problems are how to distribute the population increase from 12 million in 1964 to an expected 18–20 million by AD 2000; and secondly, how to resolve the competition for space and the resultant sprawling urban growth. If nothing is done, the result could be a curvi-linear city 110 miles long; the agricultural heartland of the ring could fill up rapidly and become a formless sprawl, a Dutch Los Angeles.

Rhine–Ruhr

The Rhine–Ruhr is also a complex polycentric metropolis. Its origins began with the settlement of populations near a concentration of overland routes, coal resources, and water transport. Then came a huge influx of workers to man the iron and steel mills of the big capitalists Thyssen and Krupp. Today the Rhine–Ruhr plays a dominant role in national production. It produces four fifths of the nation's hard coal and three fifths of its steel, and is an important economic centre of the Common Market.

Its constituent parts are: Bonn, the political and university capital; Cologne, headquarters of several federal departments, a leading financial centre, and site of the Bayer chemical works, refineries, and petro-chemical works; Düsseldorf, capital of one of the most wealthy and populous provinces, Nord-Rhein-Westphalen, and home of powerful industrial firms; Essen,

37

headquarters of mining and steel firms and organizations; plus a host of fast-growing towns.

Within a forty-mile radius of Düsseldorf live over 10 million people, or 20 per cent of the German Federal Republic. It is the greatest concentration of people on the European continent, including the Soviet Union, and is exceeded only by the London metropolitan area. There are ten cities with over 200,000 people each and another ten with between 100,000 and 200,000. According to an article by Professor Gerd Alberts of the Technische Hochschule, Munich,

Migration has tended strongly towards these areas – mainly filling in the built inner areas in the first decade after the war, and later directed towards the outer fringes. Rising land values, increasing difficulties to assemble and redevelop land in towns, federal housing and taxing policy, and a large increase in the use of cars all contributed to this development which caused a considerable spread of most towns.

As a result there is a heavy demand for limited space. Built-up areas are growing without adequate co-ordinated planning control. Labour shifts from the declining coal-fields create gaps in the manpower system. New types of industries are needed to replace obsolescent ones and to provide new jobs. The road transport system is overloaded and must be replanned and rebuilt.

In Germany today [writes Professor Alberts] the emphasis is not on the need to replace unfit habitations, important though this may be, but rather on the more fundamental question how to restructure the overall settlement pattern and its elements in urban and rural areas in a way which corresponds to the requirements of society.

The Challenge of Megalopolis

The growth of metropolitan regions, it is clear, is not an isolated phenomenon. It occurs as cities and national economies compete for industrial and political power and access to consumer markets. The Golden Triangle of Europe, an area including Birmingham, London, Paris, Brussels, Antwerp, the Randstad, the Rhine–Ruhr, Bonn, and Frankfurt, provides a case in point. Competition among these cities is keen. London's key position in the Triangle's trading economy is particularly threatened; her role as a port and trading entrepôt has been equalled or surpassed by European mainland ports like Antwerp, Rotterdam, and Hamburg. They have forged ahead with technological improvements for large-scale handling of bulk cargo, e.g. containerization, and have received massive government assistance. As a result they have been able to lower their costs and have prised loose Britain's grip on transport of primary bulk commodities, such as oil and grain.

Map 2: The Golden Triangle

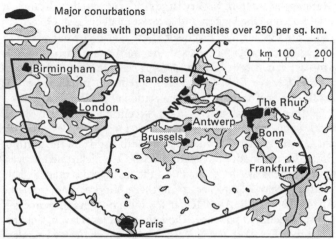

Source: *New Society*, 14 May 1970, p. 82.

In manufacturing, since the Second World War, cities on the coastline of northwestern Europe from Dunkirk to Hamburg have attracted iron, steel, chemical, and aluminium industries. Currently, for example, two new steel plants are proposed in Holland at Maasvlakte – the seaward extension of Rotterdam's Europort. Meanwhile, British policy on the location of industry has denied such development to London and the southeast England region; thus many British-based manufacturing firms are attracted to the expanding production centres and market across the Channel.

Movement of capital, labour, and resources around the Golden Triangle encourages the growth and fusion of existing settlements. This trend will continue. Future metropolitan growth will be determined to a large extent by economic factors such as transport costs and trade barriers affecting the regional and international

39

movement of resources. Of paramount importance will be the effects on city growth of the future political and economic development of the European Common Market.

The growth and fusion of cities as a part of a general pattern of twentieth-century economic expansion heralds the coming into existence of a new urban form, megalopolis, the giant city of cities. The word is of Greek origin and was coined two and a half thousand years ago when a group of philosophers and statesmen planned a new city-state in the Peloponnese. They called it Megalopolis, meaning 'a very large city', because they dreamed it would become the biggest and greatest of all cities in Greece. In 1961 Jean Gottmann, a professor at the University of Paris and a distinguished geographer, used the word again in his massive 810-page report called *Megalopolis: The Urbanized Northeastern Seaboard of the United States.* He predicted it would be 'the cradle of a new order in the organization of inhabited space'.

Gottmann's megalopolis is an almost continuous string of central cities, suburbs, and satellite areas stretching 450 miles along the old U.S. Highway 1 on the Atlantic seaboard from the north of Boston to the south of Washington, D.C. – nicknamed irreverently the 'Bos-Wash'. It includes the major cities ranging from southern New Hampshire to northern Virginia and from the Atlantic shore to the Appalachian foothills: Boston and Worcester, Massachusetts; Providence, Rhode Island; New Haven, Connecticut; the New York, New York–Newark, New Jersey complex; Trenton, New Jersey; Philadelphia and Chester, Pennsylvania; Wilmington, Delaware; Baltimore, Maryland; and Washington, D.C.

The 'Bos-Wash' had an estimated population in 1960 of nearly 40 million people living in an area of 53,000 square miles, at a density of 700 persons per square mile or fourteen times the national average. The land is divided by rivers, bays, ridges, valleys, and administrative boundaries. In it there are ten states and 117 counties plus the District of Columbia. The New York metropolitan region alone, as defined by the Regional Plan Association, includes three states, twenty-two counties, and some 1,400 local governments.

The 'Bos-Wash' is the most influential section of America and perhaps the largest, wealthiest, and most productive urbanized region on earth. Its rise to power is bound up with the emergence between the two world wars of America as the financial and productive giant and creditor of the world. It is the Main Street of the nation and makes and consumes everything from aeroplanes to zippers. It holds a pre-eminent position in finance, government, manufacture, university, and science-based industries. It contains the richest fifth of the nation's population on only a thousandth part of the land.

Map 3: The 'Bos-Wash', U.S.A. East Coast Megalopolis

Source: Wolf Von Eckardt, *The Challenge of Megalopolis*, based on the original study of Jean Gottmann (The Macmillan Company, 1964).

Great strides have been made in conquering diseases, reducing infant mortality, and in creating the goods and symbols of affluence: interior heating, air conditioning, and a thousand and one different comforts. But when people step out of their homes and apartments they enter an environment which is polluted by 'the mess that is man-made America': overflowing dustbins and huge refuse heaps; intense motorized living, though with traffic

41

rarely moving freely and speedily; huge deficit losses by transit systems; vast areas of slums and dereliction; widespread poverty and welfare-supported families.

Deep in the heart of the industrial Midwest another American city of cities is also in formation. It is the Great Lakes Megalopolis situated south of Lake Michigan, Lake Huron, and Lake Erie, and extending from Milwaukee to Pittsburgh. It has a total population of 36 million and consists of four main urban clusters: Milwaukee–Chicago, Detroit, Cleveland, and Pittsburgh, with many smaller clusters appearing as extensions or dependencies of the larger ones.

Map 4: Great Lakes Megalopolis

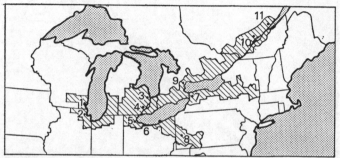

1. Milwaukee   4. Detroit   6. Cleveland   8. Pittsburgh   10. Montreal
2. Chicago   5. Toledo   7. Buffalo   9. Toronto   11. Quebec
3. Port Huron

Source: 'Into the 21st Century'. The story of the developing urban Detroit area, a report prepared by the Detroit Edison Company, October 1969.

The urban Detroit area with an estimated 8 million people is situated at the centre of the Great Lakes megalopolis. Its size is enormous by any standard; it extends over twenty-five counties in Michigan, nine in Ohio, and three in Canada and covers 23,059 square miles. Its problems of growth and development are enormous also, but with a special socio-economic twist. The urban Detroit area specializes in the production of durable consumer goods, especially automotive vehicles. It has the fastest growth of production in periods of economic prosperity, but with a depression or recession production declines rapidly, workers are laid off, and families starve or queue up for welfare hand-outs, as happened during the bitter years of the Great Depression of the 1930s.

This new American giant city has come under the scrutiny of one of the world's foremost planners, Dr Constantinos A. Doxiadis. In his book *Emergence and Growth of an Urban Region*, he attempts a definition of megalopolis which, though ponderously expressed, distinguishes certain crucial characteristics of the megalopolitan urban phenomenon.

Megalopolis is a multi-nucleated band formation, each nucleus of which, comprising at least one major urban centre, usually consists of a 'cluster' or 'constellation' of settlements of varying nature and arrangement. The nuclei are arranged along a main axis, and are interconnected by a system of interactions and flows at a level which exceeds the metropolitan one. It is this last feature that typically confers the megalopolitan character on the whole formation.

Map 5: Urban Detroit Area

Source: 'Into the 21st Century'. The story of the developing urban Detroit area, a report prepared by the Detroit Edison Company, October 1969.

Dr Doxiadis, who won his reputation for ingenuity and far-sightedness with a number of seminal essays on Ekistics, a new science of human settlements, also predicts the formation of three additional broad areas of growth in North America: the areas of Florida, the Gulf of Mexico, and the Canadian megalopolis along

43

the St Lawrence Seaway. (All of them, interestingly enough, border on large bodies of water while, he argues, the areas of urban decline are inland.) He speculates as well about the future beyond the twenty-first century when the three big megalopolises (Great Lakes, 'Bos-Wash', and St Lawrence Seaway) merge and, with the inevitable in-filling of industries and houses, become the world's first and largest complex of megalopolises.

In many other parts of the world, major cities and their regions are steadily merging across hundreds of miles into large continuous settlements. In Europe, if the growth of cities and their residential and industrial suburbs continues, we may one day see a megalopolis stretching from London and the northerly English conurbations across the Channel to the Randstad cities in the Netherlands and down through the Rhine–Ruhr region to the southern edge of Germany. By AD 3000 the world's megalopolitan area may rise to a population of 1,500 million people, and perhaps the vast majority of the world's population will be concentrated into five or six main urbanized groups.

If current trends continue the urban explosion will grow in intensity. Perhaps, sometime in the yet dim future, all the giant cities and urban regions may coalesce into a single world-encompassing city leaping across historic natural and political barriers to enclose virtually all of mankind on only a fraction of the earth's land surface. This world-city will be a revolutionary transformation in the form and structure of human settlements and will have concussive ripple effects upon the habitat, economy, and ways of life of all mankind. No one knows whether human nature will be able to withstand or adapt to so radical and rapid a change. But one thing is sure, future generations will live within and have to come to terms with the awesome growth possibilities of urban and megalopolitan societies with all their associated social, political, and economic problems.

44

2   Slums and Suburbs

Over most of man's history 90 per cent of the world's population have lived in rural areas. Three quarters of them still do. But, as we have seen, this will not last for long. For, over the next forty years, if the pattern of rural decline and industrial development is maintained, hundreds of millions will pour into urban areas in search of jobs and housing.

This massive concentration of people in cities will intensify the bitter competition for space. Urban land is scarce and expensive. How it is used, and whether it gets used for factories, offices, roads, schools, or housing – or lies vacant – depends on money and the manipulation of power in urban politics. The prospect for better housing is especially grim. Housing which average workers can afford is old and dwindling rapidly as changing land uses eat up space in central areas. The cost of renting, buying, and providing housing spirals upwards as landowners and private interest play a restrictive high-priced game of Monopoly in the property market.

Two things are bound to happen. More people will crowd into already congested substandard housing. Blight and neglect will send whole areas plummeting slumwards. And, in turn, middle-income families searching for better housing at moderate costs will flee towards the suburbs. Eventually, as suburban densities rise, the city's perimeter will be pushed outwards in a chaotic sprawling mess. These powerful forces – obsolescence in central city slums and sprawling suburbs – are two fundamental but often misunderstood aspects of the urban crisis.

What Is a Slum?

The word 'slum' was used in the 1800s as a term for squalid housing in densely populated districts of industrial cities. Today it describes poor housing and social conditions of every kind – from a spacious Boston mansion cut up into furnished rooms-to-let, to a flattened Esso petrol drum sheltering a dockworker's family in Porto-Novo, Dahomey. Urban slums are a worldwide problem, as common in the great and not-so-great cities of Europe and North America as they are in the new nations of the Third World. They can be found in the congested old quarters of European cities like Rome and Lisbon, in newly built low-quality housing in Naples, in the black ghettos of Newark, New Jersey, and the large Victorian dwellings of central London abandoned by the middle classes. Slums come in all sizes, shapes, and forms. They can be rented or owner-occupied, legally or illegally. Anything from a single family to a score of itinerant workers may live in them.

Everywhere the physical characteristics of slums are depressingly similar: poor-quality buildings, unhealthy environments, and overcrowding. In Paris one quarter of the 3·2 million dwellings are overcrowded. Tenement areas in the East End – the traditional home of the Parisian poor – are under stress. Mexico City's poor, recruited from all the impoverished regions of the country, live in one-room hovels amidst factories and warehouses, refuse heaps and littered muddy streets, crumbling churches and makeshift taverns selling *pulque*, a native drink. Thousands of slum dwellers near the wharves of Oporto, one of Portugal's major seaports, live without electricity, sanitation, or running water.

In Moscow Soviet authorities are still tackling problems of overpopulated old housing inherited from pre-revolutionary days, while faced with the increasingly strident demands of a growing population for better conditions. At the same time in the towns of the Soviet hinterlands like the Uzbekistan Republic, the housing situation remains far below standard; in one town, Tashkent, about 25 per cent of the population live in mud houses. In Tokyo crowded poor-quality housing nestles near modern science-based factories. Homeless families bombed out during the Second World War still live in boats, unused railway carriages, and abandoned factories. A third of the city dwellings have no sewerage and rely on 'night soil' men to collect excreta and dump it in the Pacific Ocean.

Slums are residential areas so physically and socially deteriorated as to make satisfactory family life impossible. Typically,

46

families live in unfit structures in disrepair. Health and safety are constantly menaced by lack of air, light, ventilation, toilet, and bathing facilities. But more important than this is the volatile but little-understood factor of congestion – the pressure of far too many people in too little space – without privacy and access to recreational amenities.

Population density and pathological behaviour are definitely linked. This is a well-known fact. When mice, for example, are placed in cages and left to struggle for food, they respond to the growth in their numbers with abnormal behaviour. Adults constantly fight, mothers kill and eat their children. Similarly, when a community of rats, usually accommodated in a small laboratory habitat, doubled their numbers without any increase in living space, females failed to carry their pregnancies to full term or to survive the delivery of their litters. Males were tense, overactive, and aggressive. Some fought and ate their weaker opponents; others hid under heaving piles of bodies and emerged to eat, drink, and move about only when other members of the community were asleep.

Among humans the direct effect of overcrowded environments is yet to be fully established. But the indirect results lead to ill-health, family conflicts, and personality disorders. When large numbers of families share toilets and baths, and have no place to keep food, infectious and digestive diseases follow. Injuries occur in cramped cooking quarters. Inadequate heating, ventilation, and bedroom space lead to tiredness and irritation. Individuals under stress have no place to retreat from the buzzing confusion of crowded households. Their lives are distorted by the bitterness of unrelieved frustration and despair.

The people of the slums are not randomly distributed across the urban landscape. They live in four major zones: squalid tenements and working-men's houses without toilets and baths; twilight zones of overcrowded and decaying ex-middle-class housing; the 'urban villages' or ghettos of colour, kith, and kin which have names like 'Little Italy', 'Villejuif', 'Black Belt', or 'Spanish Harlem'; and finally in the third-class commercial areas – the 'urban jungle' or Skid Row of single men, transients, purveyors of illicit but desired services, down-and-outers, and the chronically unemployed.

Slums are a way of being in darkness while the rest of society is bathed in light. Many people live in them, and those who have escaped still wrestle with their memories of deprivation. What is life in slums like? Public welfare workers know; they go into them, and so do firemen, policemen, journalists, and building inspectors. A few dedicated clergymen, bill collectors, and vote-seeking politicians may also venture inside sometimes. From them we get most of our views, images, and stereotypes about the darkened surroundings, pungent smells of urine and cooking, soot-laden air, and the snotty-nosed children of poor families. 'Slum' when looked at more closely is an evaluative word. Although it is often defined in quantitative terms, it serves as well to express one's attitudes. 'Slums', 'slummy', 'slumminess' – it is easy to slip into a moral position about 'those people', those 'lower classes'. And when combined with maxims like 'birds of a feather flock together' the word slum becomes an excuse for relegating the poor to the dark corners of society's conscience.

Slums Grow

Slums do not appear and disappear without cause. They exist because no urban industrial society provides the masses of its workers with access to the full benefits of their labour – good housing at reasonable prices, education, and an increasing freedom of choice. Slums spread and grow menacingly larger at critical moments in history when rapidly changing societies pull people to cities and the competition for space relegates the poorest and weakest into the worst housing.

In European nations millions of migrating workers from declining mining and farming regions converge on the fast-growing manufacturing and service centres, at home and abroad. The migrant stream originates in the poorer areas of southern European and Mediterranean countries like Yugoslavia, Greece, Portugal, and Italy, which provide 80 per cent of all migrant labour in six nations of the European Economic Community. They are headed towards the major industrial regions of France, West Germany, Belgium, and the Netherlands. Five million of them are already in the job markets of the European Community, and millions more are criss-crossing national boundaries in search of work and living quarters. This massive influx of workers, in some cases as high as 10 or 20 per cent of the host's national labour force, plays havoc with unresolved housing

Table 5

Stock of Dwellings in the European Economic Community

Country	Year (end)	Dwellings ('000s)	Number of dwellings per 1,000 population	Of which built		House-building programme (number of dwellings to be built annually in the medium term)
				Before 1945 %	Before 1914 %	
Belgium	1968	3,493·5	362·7	71	47	60,000
Germany	1968	20,596·6	340·4	50	33	500,000
France	1968	18,256·1	377·9	72	47	510,000
Italy	1969	16,822·4	315·1	54	—	460,000 (est.)
Luxembourg	1968	106·0	315·1	60	—	2,000
Netherlands	1969	3,687·4	284·8	54	28	125,000/130,000 (approx.)
						Community 1,660,000 (approx.)

Estimate of Number of Slum Dwellings and Number of Dwellings Requiring Modernization in the Community Countries

Belgium: 400,000 dwellings are regarded as slums to be demolished. 600,000 dwellings require modernization.

Germany: 7 million of the 10 million dwellings built before 1948 need to be replaced or modernized.

France: 7·5 million dwellings fall below the elementary standards of modern comfort. From 1970 onwards, some 200,000 old premises will be improved each year.

Italy: Several million dwellings need to be modernized.

Netherlands: Of the 1,900,000 dwellings built before 1946, 350,000 must be regarded as slums and 250,000 as dwellings which can be improved.

Source: *Social Statistics Year Book 1970*, Statistical Office of the European Communities.

problems. Recent estimates based on 1968-9 survey data indicate that major urban centres of the community have huge housing deficits and a massive backlog of slum dwellings and houses in need of repair and modernization. National figures give some idea of the scale of the problem: 47 per cent of the 3·4 million dwellings in Belgium and of the 18·2 million dwellings in France were built before 1914 and have reached the end of their useful life. The same is true of a third of Germany's 20·5 million dwellings.

In Britain the quest for rapid economic growth has exposed the inadequacies of housing. New roads, industrial buildings, and transport systems come first in the long queue for scarce land resources. Millions of migrating workers drawn from the poorer regions of the nation, Europe, and the Commonwealth compete with local residents for housing that is already in short supply. The national housing stock is old and badly distributed, and 20 per cent of all households live at or below barely acceptable levels of poverty.

The situation in America, one of the wealthiest nations in the world, is no better. Postwar economic changes and the growth of science and military-based industries have attracted vast numbers of country dwellers into cities. Today 70 per cent of all Americans live in urban areas, and by the end of this century cities will have to provide 2 million new homes a year, schools for 10 million additional children, welfare and health facilities for 3 million elderly persons, and transport for the daily movement of 200 million people and more than 80 million cars. At the same time there is a pressing need for major urban surgery to overcome decay. To meet these challenges America will have to build in its cities as much again in forty years as has been built since the first colonists arrived on the New England coast three centuries ago.

Trouble certainly lies ahead in America. Over 9 million homes are run down and deteriorating. More than 4 million do not have running water or even plumbing. All told, a quarter of the entire population lives in an estimated 15·7 million slum or near-slum dwellings. Bad housing and poverty go together. Two fifths of the people live at or below accepted minimum standards of decency and the bottom fifth subsist on annual incomes far below the level of the national average income. In a country where a round-trip air ticket from New York to sunny California costs about $300, a modest car costs $2,500, and a single year of college education costs $4,000, poverty means blocked opportunity. A large proportion of the people do not have access to higher education and mobility – the things that matter in American society.

Similar pressures and problems abound in rapidly growing cities of the developing nations: Buenos Aires, Mexico City, Rio de Janeiro and São Paulo, Cairo, Calcutta, Bombay, and Hong Kong. In Calcutta, for example, more than 7 million people now live in the 400-square-mile metropolitan district. It is India's largest urban centre and serves the nation as an important seaport, and diversified manufacturing and governmental centre. The earth is a flat, wet delta land. Networks of dark green trees and coconut palms, interspersed with shallow ponds, follow the slow bendings of rivers. Poverty-stricken villages huddle together on the fringes of the city, shanties crowd the airport road. The centre is heavily congested at the banks of the Hooghly River, particularly at each end of the Howrah Bridge, and wharf roofs and factories stretch like a broad, dirty ribbon for miles up- and down-stream from the heart of the metropolis.

The major cities of the world are dying at the core. Physical and social obsolescence in their central areas is growing rapidly and casts a pall of ugliness and despair over the spirits of the people. In terms of the future two prospects face newcomers seeking jobs and homes in the inner city – either success and movement up the socio-economic scale and out to the suburbs, or a slow spiral downwards to social and personal oblivion.

Suburbs Scatter

The changing and churning within modern cities spills over the edges of the congested inner areas into the suburbs, fills in the empty spaces, and heads out into the countryside. The major causes are the movement of people, commerce, and industry. Rail lines extend urban growth along main radial arteries. Buses and motor-cars fill in the spaces where single semi-detached houses are spread out at fairly low densities. White-collar workers – professionals, managers, and well-paid office staff – are the trend-setters. Commerce and light industry follow not far behind this affluent consumer market and skilled labour force.

This sets off a chain reaction. New jobs attract more workers, particularly semi-skilled persons, and more cars and roads, and more factories and large shopping centres. And so it goes on. Today the frontiers of building are rapidly pushing outwards and the newer suburbs at the fringe are growing faster than any other area of the city.

Suburbs are usually defined as residential districts on or near the outskirts of town. Typically, they represent the latest layer of housing built at lower densities to meet the demands of middle-income families for space. Suburbs are not static, however; they are a constantly evolving aspect of urban growth. As the growing city overtakes and populates the outer layer more densely, another layer is added, farther out, by a new generation of suburbanites and it becomes 'the suburbs'. 'Almost every part of any city was at one time a suburb,' says Peter Hall in his book *World Cities*: 'Fleet Street in London, the Châtelet in Paris, Unter den Linden in Berlin, were all once *in suburbio*.'

Suburbs are not a new aspect of urban life. Throughout history wealthy people have valued a place in the country. In ancient Greece schools and sanitoria were sited outside the city. In the 1700s suburban living was the symbol of middle-class gentility and offered a retreat to nature from the competition, vulgarity, and ceaseless labour of city life. By the 1800s, however, suburbs lost much of their rustic flavour and became a diffuse mass caught up in the tentacles of the expanding city. In this context 'mass' is the key word. Twentieth-century suburbanization – the massive growth of suburbs – was related to new ideas of popular democracy, new fast methods of public transport, and increasing affluence among a new middle class made up of white-collar workers, technicians, and professionals. The result was whole areas constructed on the edges of cities composed of 'a multitude of uniform, unidentifiable houses, lined up inflexibly, at uniform distances, on uniform roads, in a treeless communal waste', as Lewis Mumford observes in his book *The City in History*. Inside the suburbs man lost his identity in the monotonous detail of his surroundings. Houses, as Mumford goes on to say, were

inhabited by people of the same class, the same income, the same age group, witnessing the same television performances, eating the same tasteless prefabricated foods, from the same freezers, conforming in every outward and inward respect to a common mould, manufactured in the central metropolis.

52

What is new in all this is our recognition that the craze for speed and mobility and the romantic notion of peaceful suburban life do not fit together. If man's huge appetite for space is not restricted, two new phenomena will occur about which we know very little. One is whole cities becoming, like Los Angeles, a sprawling chaotic mass of sameness. The other is the merging of many cities, their suburbs and outlying towns, into a giant city covering several hundreds of miles. Both possibilities cast before them the spectre of huge communities of people whose lives are purposeless, joyless, and filled with the tedium of conformity.

Los Angeles, built up after the Second World War as a motorized city, is a case of space-eating with a vengeance. Two thirds of the city area is occupied by streets, roads, parking, and garages. People make do with the remaining third. 'Spread City', as it has been called, is cut up by multi-lane highways, and the residential areas between them are clouded by smog. The 'ultimate solution', for tidy minds, will be the wholesale eviction of inhabitants in favour of the robot and machine.

London's suburbs began as large areas of semi-detached housing built within the city limits between five and fifteen miles from the centre. They were built at a fairly low density of ten to fifteen dwellings per acre and serviced by ordinary city transport facilities. Later, with the growth and extension of rail systems, housing estates were built farther out, some twenty to forty miles from Piccadilly Circus. The first suburbanites were well-to-do professional men and white-collar workers, all people with steady jobs who could afford to pay higher rents and rail fares. More recently, local authority resettlement schemes opened up the suburbs to the homeless and poorer families of the manual and semi-skilled workers cleared from the worst inner-city slums.

Movement to the suburbs from the inner city is generally synonymous with achieving better education and a secure well-paid job. Working-class families often show a marked change in behaviour as they enter the suburban property-owning democracy. A classic study by Peter Willmott and Michael Young of families moving from Bethnal Green to Woodford – from the slums of London's East End to the outer suburbs of the city – seems to bear this out. The rented dwellings they left were old and densely packed; more than 40,000 people were packed into 760 acres at a density of sixty-four to the acre. Noise and dirt assailed the ears and eyes. Factories and heavy traffic competed with the residents for scarce space. Close family ties and neighbours provided the intimacy that made life acceptable. In the morning, after their grim-faced cloth-capped men had trudged off to work, mothers out shopping chatted on busy street corners and their children playing hide and seek darted among the cars and market stalls.

Woodford, on the other hand, had more living space for families and a different, more genteel style of life. It had once been an old settlement of rural gentry which slowly evolved into a middle-class suburb. In it 61,000 people lived on 3,841 acres, at a density of only sixteen people per acre. The well-kept residences, lawns and gardens enclosed by hedges, marked each man's home as his own castle. Newcomers feel like strangers in their new surroundings and are quiet and reserved in public. The informal friendliness of the old neighbourhood is gone, but the families feel satisfied that they have made a step up the ladder of success and self-respect.

Modern suburbanization in Paris was, as elsewhere, a complex social process. It enlarged the privileges of the new middle class and produced a new way of life. Many French suburbanites work in large central-city businesses, government offices, cultural establishments, and scientific institutes. Unlike their city cousins, they are purged of partisan passions. They renounce romanticism and political idealism in favour of security and material goals.

The suburbanization of Paris accompanied the French Industrial Revolution. Each successive wave of building produced a growing mixture of housing types: Gothic 1880, Renaissance 1890, and Châteaux 1900. There were mansions, Basque villas, Tudor replicas, and Swiss chalets. Between the two world wars a delirium of building abandoned all pretence of architectural quality or originality. Whole areas were given over to mass-produced housing for families of moderate means, and here and there among them in their 'pavilions' and 'villas' lived the well-to-do classes. In the Paris suburbs, from Issy-les-Moulineaux to Drancy, Levallois-Perret to Villemomble, and from Kremlin-Bicêtre to Pantin, one can see the small detached houses each with a fence, iron gate, and little patch of land for gardening and tinkering.

Dramatic changes occurred in the post-1945 period. The urban population explosion, the building of huge multiple dwellings, and the increasing numbers of cars populated the suburbs more and more densely. The few remaining park areas – the last shaded refuges – were studded with enormous apartment-house complexes. These towers overshadowed the miniature world of the one-storey house and pavilion, and produced what has been called 'the ugliness of the very little and the too big'. Bare façades are profiled against formless landscapes. Bands of well-groomed children roam the unfinished and unnamed streets. Outwardly they are symbols of the new middle-class respectability; inside they are bored and disillusioned.

The Paris suburb moved into the second half of the twentieth century with a portmanteau of anarchy and ugliness. And now a new kind of housing is about to be added. Levitt & Sons – builders of the Levittown suburbs on the East Coast of the United States – has launched a campaign to build well-equipped, single-family houses grouped around modern community facilities. By adapting home interiors to meet French cultural patterns – isolating the kitchen from the dining room and enlarging the bathroom to accommodate the bidet, and offering a full range of amenities – Levitt hopes to create a new market and a new type of neighbourly community. Despite these innovations, which may appeal to the adventurous and wealthy, most people will probably still choose to live in apartment houses; and planners are contemplating building 'skyscraper cities' on the outskirts of the many city areas to accommodate the huge population increase expected over the next thirty years.

The classic example of mass suburbanization in the United States is New York City. It is the largest urban settlement in the United States and the centre of a huge three-state Eastern Seaboard region encompassing New York, New Jersey, and Connecticut. Rapid suburbanization took place in the late 1940s outside the city limits some fifteen to twenty-five miles from Times Square. Residents depended on commuter trains and cars, in contrast to London where suburbs were inside the city and serviced by rapid public transit. The New York suburbs were built with very low densities – seven houses per acre with room for garages, lawns, and gardens. Residents worked in or near Manhattan Island and many of them commuted from home to work by car and rail. By the 1950s the suburbs had spread relentlessly around Manhattan. In the new outer zone – some twenty-five to fifty miles from Times Square – houses were spread still farther apart on single plots of land up to two thirds of an acre in size. Today suburbs form part of a fifty-mile semicircle around New York City encompassing an area of almost 7,000 square miles, and housing more than 16 million people.

The implications of this growth are disturbing. Peter Hall, a leading British geographer, has calculated the likely devastating results and issued a warning to American planners. In 1960 out of a total of 6,900 square miles in the New York metropolitan region, 2,400 were developed or committed to open space or some other public use. But given the likely increase of population between 1960 and 1985, and the present zoning arrangements, future development could eat up another 2,800 square miles. In the process, New York might well use up more land than in all the years since 1626, when Manhattan was bought from the Indians for twenty-four dollars. The result would be continuous sprawl stretching up to fifty miles from Times Square.

Farther out in the outlying rural areas around New York, which some sociologists call exurbia, adventurous and affluent families are searching for peace and quiet. They are, unwittingly, the pioneers of an urban sprawl without parallel on the Eastern Seaboard. Many 'exurbanites' are well-to-do owners of fashionable homes and two-car garages. They tend to live in villages and small established communities. Rail networks are far away and bus transport is inadequate so families depend entirely on their cars. Commuters bound for New York start their journey with a long drive to the rail station; and wives must have a second car for long journeys to schools and shopping centres. Densities are low, relative to the suburbs, but still ten times higher than the surrounding countryside. Despite the affluence of residents, however, exurban communities are not without their problems. Local municipal income from property taxes is unable to support the demand for top-level educational facilities. So families with young schoolchildren leave. Arguments break out when residents debate zoning laws limiting the influx of newcomers, or encouraging the location of light industry, research organizations, and offices to gain new revenue.

Levittown, a new community in Willingboro, New Jersey, provides a good portrait of social conflict in American suburban communities. It has merit also as an example of the megalopolitan in-filling process taking place on the fringe of the New York City tri-state region not far from the suburbs of Philadelphia, the fourth largest urban agglomeration in America.

Levittown was conceived and built by Levitt & Sons, a company founded during the depression. Levitt made his money building suburban subdivisions in Long Island for upper-middle-class families. Then in two new communities in New York and Pennsylvania he established what has become a typical pattern of privately built housing development. The company bought land, built small cheaper versions of upper-income houses, and added in the bargain modern appliances, village greens, and community facilities.

Levittown, New Jersey, the third project, was planned as a community of 12,000 houses ranging in price from $11,500 to $14,500. In addition, for the first time, residents were offered their own township government. This novel community attracted the attention of a sociologist, Herbert Gans, who lived there in 1958. His study of the Levittowners and how the first families coped with the demands of community self-government makes fascinating reading. Three quarters of the Levittowners were drawn from the middle and lower-middle American social classes. There were white-collar workers – managers and minor officials, technicians and semi-professionals – and blue-collar representatives of the skilled manual workers like foremen, printers, electricians, and plumbers. About 20 per cent of the remainder were working class, and 5 to 10 per cent were professional men and businessmen. There was a mixture, too, of ethnic and religious backgrounds: a few so-called 'WASPS' – the long-established families of white Anglo-Saxon Protestants of English, German, and Scandinavian origins who are America's high-status social group – many Irish and Italian Catholics, East Europeans and Russian Jews, and a handful of Greeks, Asians, and black Americans.

Faced with a need to develop a sense of community consciousness in order to make Levittown work in human terms, the residents found it difficult to overcome their differing backgrounds. In addition, conflicting social attitudes made communication difficult. Upper-middle-class businessmen and managers concentrated on golf and the country club. Professionals, many of them Jews, held liberal attitudes about racial and religious harmony, world peace, and the need for community planning. Many lower-middle-class persons held conservative, puritan and Calvinist views and were concerned only with respectability; others were bigoted, impulsive, and aggressive in their relations with neighbours. Levittowners just couldn't accommodate themselves to living with people who were 'different'. Each family denigrated its neighbours on grounds of race, class, or religion; and there was a constant search elsewhere for compatible acquaintances. These hostilities affected all aspects of community life and made it difficult to establish an effective township government and decision-making procedure to deal with the problems of suburban life, inadequate public finances, transportation, schools, and social services.

Slums in the Suburbs

Suburbanization is a continuous process. Movement into the suburbs from the central city stimulates movement farther out. As each area fills up, something of its former exclusiveness fades. Old-timers who had gone to the city's edge in search of greenery and seclusion move still farther out, while newcomers take their place. The long-term tendency is for the density of settlement to spread outwards. At the same time blight and neglect attack the older, now less desirable suburban areas. Larger houses are divided up into cubicles of rented accommodation. Older houses fall into disrepair and when vacated become targets for homeless families in search of shelter.

The goal of suburban life is not unique to the new affluent middle class. It is held also by poorer families in urban societies. This goal, allied with the decreasing stock of fit low-rent housing in the inner city, has triggered the poor men's trek to the suburbs. They seek shelter in the pockets of wasteland or obsolescent suburban housing. Those who can, rent; some of those who cannot are driven by their homeless plight to seize land and build makeshift housing or forcibly enter and re-use old vacant buildings.

Squatting and squatters' settlements on the edge of large cities throw a shadow over the more affluent citizens. Squatting in legal terms is the forcible occupation of private or public property. Socially, it is the occupation of vacant land or buildings by landless or homeless people in search of a haven. Squatters' settlements are generally found in the suburbs and their growth – like that of middle-class suburbs – is an aspect of the tremendous changes taking place in urban industrial and developing economies. In all the suburbs of the major cities of the world each day poor people are, in the words of one observer, 'assembling, dispersing, looking about, and betaking themselves to shelter'. Newcomers to the city and old-timers, fed up with paying exorbitant slum rents, create an 'architecture without architects', and dig in for a long battle with the authorities.

Every city has its example of 'Squattersville'. There are the *favelas* of Rio, the *colonias proletarias* of Mexico City, the *Gecekondu* of Istanbul, the *villes extra-coutumiers* of Kinshasa, Congo, the *poblaciones* of Santiago, the 'unauthorized structures' of Hong Kong and Athens, and the *bidonvilles* or tin-can cities of Nanterre and St-Denis, outside Paris. In America, black migrants to Chicago build shanties in vacant lots; and poor whites squat on newly irrigated land or forests opened up by roads along the Colorado River. London's homeless families established squatters' communes in the vacant houses of Ilford in 1969 and fought hired thugs and police for several weeks. So did the poor shanty dwellers of Rome and Milan.

The suburban *poblaciones* of Santiago de Chile are one of the most dramatic examples of squatters' settlements in the world. They are self-help uprisings that took the shape of communities built by and for the poor. The squatters' movement began in earnest in 1970 when tenement slum dwellers in central Santiago invaded government-owned land on the periphery. They constructed and occupied their homes of wood, cardboard, and mud, and defied the authorities to dislodge them. Today there are 500,000 residents of *poblaciones* – one sixth of Santiago's population of 3 million people. The bulk of them are not much different from the large mass of urban dwellers; they just got tired of waiting for the authorities to do something about their plight. Many residents have secured a place in the society as employed, literate wage-earners; over the years they convert their humble dwellings into respectable homes of brick and cement. Their confrontation with state power has had a salutary effect. The people gained self-respect and can now negotiate with the authorities as equals rather than as dependent clients. With the stabilization of life in the *poblaciones* they become part of the new suburbs, and another layer is added to the city's structure.

Hong Kong, a British colony in Asia, has achieved one of the highest rates of economic progress in the Third World. Rapid industrial growth has attracted Chinese peasants from the colony's region and neighbouring states and raised the population to more than 2·5 million. Since 1945 the population has multiplied six times. In every square mile there are more than 200,000 persons and one in every five live in illegal unregulated makeshift shelters, abandoned premises, and squatters' settlements. Hong Kong's squatters are people who have no choice but to live in a flimsy shack in a city where most privately built permanent housing is bad and costly. As in Santiago, many squatters are old-time city dwellers and are no different in social class composition than other urban residents. They have a few more children, but families are neither very rich nor very poor. People become squatters simply because there is nothing better available – and in the meantime they must carry on, they must have somewhere to rest and to live while they hope.

Athens was once a small medieval village of 5,000 people on the slopes of the Acropolis; today because of in-migration and population growth there are more than 2 million people dispersed over an area of 180 square miles. Buildings cover the land in successive tiers. As each wave of families build on the edge of the city, another tier is added. A large proportion of the suburbs are in fact illegal settlements of squatters living in 'unauthorized structures'. In them live 20 per cent of the half million entrants into the city since 1951. They are not slums in the usual sense of the word. There is a good deal of energy and creativity involved in the buildings, and families have typical middle-class outlooks on values. Squalor here is public not private. The dust-laden atmosphere and landscape dotted with refuse heaps are symptoms of uncontrolled urban sprawl and inadequate public amenities. Inside the homes there is none of the unrelieved poverty one finds among the poorest urban dwellers.

Athens' squatters can buy the land they dwell upon, although to get it they must pay exorbitant prices. And even when the land is bought, it is not easy to get permission to build on it. The only solution is to erect their simple homes secretly in the early hours of the morning or when the police are busy at festivals and public events. Two quick building types are used: a small one-room shelter to which other units are added or, more commonly, a large roofed space within which inner partitioning walls are added later. This latter technique is preferred because the structure then becomes, in the jargon of municipal administrators, 'a permanent inhabited space'. In time planning permission is given and the settlement becomes a stable area of wage-earners

60

and rising land values. Then – and only then – do the authorities deign to supply the basic public services. This process has created two Athens: the central city is 'legitimate' and many of the outer areas are 'unauthorized'. Settlers are victimized by property speculators, much capital is wasted, and the energies of planners must be spent later tidying up a chaotic mess.

Taming Decay and Sprawl

The problems of slums and suburbs are inter-related within the the whole framework of urbanization. Their solution requires a systematic, comprehensive, and planned attack from every angle: political, legal, financial, social, and educational. Today planners, architects, urban designers, and social workers are at work in all the major world cities. Spurring them on are enraged citizens' groups and harassed officials. Academic bodies, government institutions, and a host of voluntary community development agencies are beginning to provide the finance and technological armoury for what is literally a battle against decay and sprawl.

In the obsolescent inner areas the major task is urban renewal. This involves a co-ordinated comprehensive plan to undertake the revitalization of life through the upgrading of existing dwellings, the building of better-quality housing, the improvement of environments, and the increased access of lower-income families to social benefits. The accomplishment of this task lies far beyond the abilities and finances of municipal governments. It requires central government guidance and financial aid, linked with the recognition of a moral purpose.

A series of housing acts promoted by Congress in the United States provides an example of a legislative lead in slum clearance and urban redevelopment. The 1949 Act, for instance, sought to remedy the serious housing shortage, to eliminate substandard and other inadequate housing. It proposed the clearance of slums and blighted areas and set forth the goal of a decent home in a suitable living environment for every American family. The 1954 Act called for a programme of urban renewal, rehabilitation, and conservation. It also obliged local communities to combat decay through a variety of devices: improved living codes and code enforcement, local planning, long-range capital improvement programmes, neighbourhood analyses, and re-location plans. Furthermore, federal assistance was offered for comprehensive metropolitan area planning. The 1965 Housing and Urban Development Act followed this up with a proposal for grants in aid of community planning in problem areas. The 1966 Demonstration Cities and Metropolitan Development Act (the Model Cities Act) introduced a comprehensive approach to the treatment of problems of low-income urban residents. More recent acts have sought to link urban renewal with anti-poverty and social welfare programmes.

American legislation, like its counterparts in Europe, reflects to some extent the growing feeling that the progress of man is the measure of national economic and social growth. In American cities like Boston, San Francisco, New Haven, Philadelphia, and New York, some impressive gains have been made. But the 'pay-off' has not kept pace with the backlog of problems; nor has it fully anticipated population growth. And there are also many critics of the way in which American-style renewal creates huge profits for land speculators and property developers and pushes the low-income poor into equally bad adjoining areas. Herbert Gans, of the Institute for Urban Studies, University of Pennsylvania, has set down a programme of action which may become a manifesto for planners, social workers, and citizens' groups working in slum-clearance areas. His programme calls for multi-disciplinary neighbourhood studies and the evaluation of the positive and negative effects of dislocation before decisions to act. He also advocates selective rehabilitation of neighbourhood dwellings instead of wholesale demolition, rehousing for all dislocated persons, and the encouragement of home ownership through loans and improved grants.

In Britain, the Greater London Council and its constituent borough councils have proposed a Greater London Development Plan. In a popular essay about the plan called *Tomorrow's London* they outline their main objectives. They seek to create a healthy and agreeable environment with adequate spaces for work, homes, and leisure. They are concerned about maintaining and augmenting the city's historic functions while allowing for freedom of choice and change. Above all, they are searching for answers to the problems of congestion and urban sprawl.

In the 1950s Moscow faced as difficult a set of housing problems as any great nation ravaged by war. In addition, it had never before come to grips with the vast backlog of bad housing carried over from the times of the tsars. In 1956, the Twentieth Congress of the Communist Party called for an end to the housing shortage within twenty years. The target figure set for the period 1959–65 was 15 million new homes – three times the stock of homes that existed under the last tsar. By 1962, 9 million were completed at a rate of production claimed to be greater than that of America and the northwestern European countries together. The pace of this building programme reached five hundred homes a day in 1962. By then a half million Muscovites alone had moved into new homes. At this rate it was estimated that the one million new homes needed to satisfactorily house every Moscow resident would soon be met.

At the same time planners realized that maintaining satisfactory standards of living space for rehoused Soviet families was not easy. Although a separate three-room flat for each family was the national goal, according to a statement of the Deputy Chairman of the State Planning Commission in 1961, there were many cases where 'entire families are assigned to each of the rooms in new houses, so that the new flats once more turn into overcrowded dormitories with all the joyless consequences'.

Despite these difficulties, the Soviet housing drive produced extraordinary results. There were five key aspects that other nations should look at closely: a recognized challenge; clear goals; administrative and financial procedures to achieve the goals; a well-developed building technology; and, above all, the will of the people harnessed to a desire for a better life. Soviet planners believe that through these means the worst aspects of the housing shortage will soon be eliminated. By 1980 everyone will have a modern flat at a standard of less than one person per room.

Soviet planners are also experimenting with new settlement patterns and public co-operation. At the moment, in Moscow, they have opted for high-density suburbs of five-storey housing financed by contributions from members of co-operative societies and state loans. Housing estates are planned as 'units of life' – communities of 15,000–20,000 persons on between 75 and 125 acres. The estates provided for community services like restaurants, nurseries, kindergartens, workshops, swimming pools, and parks, and convenient access to local shopping and public services. Many of these ideas will be used in the construction of new urban communities called *goroda sputniki*, or satellite towns, around big cities.

Soviet housing plans for the future, published in a recent issue of the French journal *L'Architecture d'Aujourd'hui*, are certainly attractive. But there has been a good deal of criticism, both public and professional, about some of the shortcomings of Soviet planning. These include the poor quality of detailed designs, the lagging development of community services in the estates, the rigidity of housing arranged around rectangular courtyards, and spatial monotony, like that seen in Lenin Hills, Moscow's biggest housing project.

Suburbanization, for all its problems, is not a strange disease which can be banished for ever from our societies. It is a natural process in any expanding city and has many positive functions. Suburbanization promotes flexibility of growth. It allows for the circulation of social groups and the re-use of aging housing stock, thereby providing accommodation for many modest family budgets. Its major drawbacks include the growth of small, understaffed, and ill-equipped local municipalities within the city itself. These undoubtedly help local views to be heard, but their growing numbers and parochial interests often hold back efforts to deal with city-wide problems.

On the American scene, Herbert Gans discounts the notion that suburbanization will eventually eat up all open space between neighbouring cities. On the contrary, he believes there is still plenty of vacant land inside large urban regions – more than 80 per cent in the case of the 'Bos-Wash'. He sees this argument as a 'conservative' one put forward by people who in their hearts want to preserve the United States as a predominantly rural, small-town, white, and Protestant society, in which they hold political and cultural power. The main problem of suburbanization in his eyes is its virtual exclusion of low-income manual workers and cultural and racial minorities, and the formation of exclusive, affluent, and 'white-Protestants-only' colonies. The top priority, he says, should be to give the benefits of a better life, which the suburbs allow, to all city dwellers. This can be done by planning and building more and better suburbs with mixed and balanced populations. Meanwhile, in the older suburban centres, renewal and welfare programmes must be introduced to deal with the most urgent problems of blight and neglect.

Uncontrolled suburban sprawl is widely recognized, however, as a specific and unwanted aspect of modern urban growth and change. In every city, planners, municipal authorities, and enlightened citizens' groups are seeking ways to encourage more orderly forms of development. Planners are proposing more flexible zoning standards, higher population densities near transport, and wedges of green open space radiating from the centre. They use legal and administrative procedures to create pleasant environments according to standards of size, density, and spatial distribution.

Each city authority hopes to find solutions which fit the uniqueness of its own circumstances. In Los Angeles planners have accepted the existence of a motorized 'spread city' and permitted uniform low-density development punctuated here and there with parks and employment centres. Planners in Copenhagen and the Randstad cities are encouraging growth along main radial transport lines to provide speedy access to and from the centre. In between are areas of open parkland. London and Moscow are ringing suburbs with green belts and concentrating development in separate satellite towns of limited size. Planning authorities in Moscow, as in Paris, are also limiting the demands of suburban building on land resources by building at high densities in the form of multi-storey apartment blocks.

The major critical issues involved in taming central area decay and suburban sprawl relate to three fundamental points. There is a need to abolish gross housing and socio-economic injustices, to direct the economic and aesthetic management of land and environment towards social ends, and to ensure a proper balance among the many conflicting forces of urban change. Specific actions and strategies to reach these goals should emerge from a radically revised view of the city's administrative and planning structures, and the participation of the large mass of urban dwellers in the determination of the city's future in an urbanizing world.

3   Movement and Congestion

A decade ago the brilliant social critic Lewis Mumford wrote in his book *The Highway and the City*, 'Paris, Rome, and London have already duplicated the suffocating defects of New York and Chicago, and are now rapidly moving towards the fantastic frustrations of Los Angeles, Detroit and Boston.' These dire predictions conveyed in strident, almost messianic tones, expressed the concern of one seasoned observer about the dangers of 'auto-culture', *la vice américaine*. He sensed that the single-minded quest for car ownership and auto-mobility would be fatal to the quality of life in cities and to the economy and efficiency of urban transportation.

The only cure for this disease [he said] is to rebuild the whole transportation network on a new model, which will allot to each kind of vehicle, and to each service, the special task it can best perform, and will give the user a free choice between public and private means, between fast and slow methods.

The role of urban transportation, said Mumford, is to bring people and goods to places where they are needed. It should aid the settlement of the greatest variety of population and activities within limited areas and therefore widen the possibility of choice without making it necessary to travel. Economy, efficiency, and speed of movement in comfort and safety are essential. But more importantly transportation networks should provide adaptable and flexible modes of travel and land use control that fit the changing needs of urban society.

If Mumford's hopes, which many of today's harassed city dwellers share, are a hymn to the transportation systems we might have, then what exists is nothing less than a litany of chaos and disorder: rising congestion, pollution, and accidents; poor-quality public transport; wasted land resources and environmental destruction; lack of social fit; crude designs and lack of

66

public participation; discrimination against the poor and other 'transit dependants'; bureaucratic rigidity and the dictatorial abuse of power by professionals, industrialists, developers, and politicians.

Urban Transport in Crisis

New York, the great American metropolis, provides a good example of the chaotic transport situation. About 2 million people travel each day into the nine square miles that make up Manhattan's business districts: 140,000 drive there in cars; 200,000 take buses; 100,000 go by commuter railroads; and 1,400,000, the great majority, travel on the New York City owned subways. This reliance on public rapid transit systems in New York City has no parallel elsewhere in America. In the last two decades, however, the number of transit riders has decreased in the inner area and increased sharply in the outer areas, reflecting the mass exodus of white-collar and blue-collar workers from the older housing areas to new locations in the outer areas of New York City.

The city's subway system is in a constant state of near bankruptcy. Operating costs mount at the rate of 10 per cent a year and the city has to pay the difference – about $132 million – between rising costs and the revenue from fares paid. Despite the acknowledged fact that much of the city's transit system is decrepit and outmoded, planners are determined to keep it running. 'Yes, the subways are grossly over-burdened during the rushhour,' say the editors of *The Plan for New York City*, 'and they are hideous and uncomfortable at all hours. The buses are noisy and their schedules are erratic. It is astonishing that we have managed to create a system that is such an affront to the senses. But it works.'

According to the Plan, New York City is committed to a massive $2 billion investment for mass transit and commuter rail transport improvement to bring people from outlying areas to the business districts. The major goals are: to speed up train service and improve standards of design and maintenance; to begin a massive construction programme; to air condition trains and clean up stations; and to extend subways to outlying areas

67

of northeast Bronx, outer Queens, and outer Brooklyn not presently served by public transit.

Also proposed is a cross-town link at 48th Street which will service that new West Side commercial redevelopment area, the midtown corridor of offices, superliner terminal and convention centre, and inter-connect on the East Side with the Second Avenue subway and the new Long Island Rail Road terminus. These proposals are to be augmented by plans to lure motorists out of their cars. This will require development of other bankrupt mass transit and commuter rail lines: the Trans-Hudson Tube system, the Long Island Rail Road, the Penn Central Railroad, and the Erie–Lackawanna Railway.

New York City's transit planners no doubt gaze with envy at the Lindenwold suburban line which serves Philadelphia and according to all reports has successfully converted motorists to rail commuting. The railroad thrusts through a string of communities in a fast-growing suburban belt that reaches towards the New Jersey shore. It begins as a subway in the centre of Philadelphia, and after four stops crosses the Delaware River on the Benjamin Franklin bridge. After two more subway stops in Camden, it emerges from the tunnels and continues at grade level and on embankments or slender concrete elevated structures past five suburban stations to Lindenwold, New Jersey. The $14\frac{1}{2}$-mile trip takes twenty-two minutes and fares range from 30 to 60 cents. Trains are fast, comfortable, and frequent, and the patronage of 33,400 daily riders covers the operating costs. But more importantly, the line has measurably reduced auto traffic, particularly at peak rush hours. According to surveys taken by the Delaware River Port Authority, which owns the line, 40 per cent of the riders formerly drove into the city. Now they park their cars in the 8,800 parking spaces at the line's stations.

Accomplishing a complete harmonization of urban transportation in New York will be made difficult because of the proliferation of many different and conflicting transport authorities. The city owns the subway system, which handles the bulk of daily commuters. But the feeder transport links into the city are owned, controlled, and regulated by more than twelve competing private enterprises and city, state, and federal government agencies. They include the Port Authority of New York and New Jersey, the Triborough Bridge and Tunnel Authority, the state and federal highway authorities, toll highway agencies, suburban railroads and bus lines, the New York City Transit Authority, the three state transportation regulation authorities, and the Interstate Commerce Commission.

On the streets of New York, especially downtown Manhattan, (congestion and pollution are major problems. New York City's trucks, an essential medium of goods transport, especially for the profitable garment industry, are getting larger and noisier.) In recent years, use of five-axle semi-trailer trucks in the New York region has risen from 0·5 per cent of the total semi-trailer traffic to 18 per cent, and the tonnage carried has risen even more sharply. Private automobiles operate inefficiently in city traffic. They make up 30 per cent of the vehicles moving on the streets, but account for only 8 per cent of the passenger trips into and within the midtown core. Half of all vehicles moving on midtown streets are taxis – and planners are doubtful about what to do with them. On the positive side, they carry twice as many persons as do private cars, but they require further regulation, improvements, and wider dispersal around the city. Farther out from the centre, commuter traffic on the high-speed expressways that serve the city is reaching saturation and there are new proposals to take the pressure off the congested New Jersey Turnpike, the Long Island Expressway, the Garden State Parkway in New Jersey, and the Cross-Bronx Expressway from the George Washington Bridge to the Throgs Neck Bridge.

Air congestion over New York's Kennedy and La Guardia airports is a menace also. Sheer volume of traffic is the major cause of the crisis. Whereas in 1948, Kennedy, La Guardia, and Newark airports were handling 3·6 million passengers a year, by 1968 they were handling ten times that number. And none too well. 'Hold' areas over the region are saturated with incoming planes waiting their turn to land, and long delays of outgoing planes occur with increasing frequency. But there is little chance that these problems will be resolved any time soon. The reason is that the air industry is one of New York's fastest-growing industries. It provides 55,000 jobs at the airports alone, with a payroll of over $550 million a year. New plans are to expand runways into Jamaica Bay, to build a fourth jetport, and to introduce innovations in air-cargo handling which has grown rapidly into a $6·8 billion industry.

Britain is still at a comparatively early stage in the Motor Age, asserted Professor Colin Buchanan in his famous study *Traffic in Towns*, 'but we are approaching the crucial point when the ownership of private motor vehicles instead of being the privilege of a minority, becomes the expectation of the majority'. At present, in Britain, he said, there are about 16·4 million families and 6·6 million cars and 1·8 million motorcycles. But there will be a flood of cars in the next few decades. It would be a mistake, however, he cautioned his readers, for those who would compare our situation with that of America to say 'things won't be like that here'. In more respects than not, predicted the Professor of Transport at Imperial College of Science and Technology, they are likely to be very much the same.

Since 1964 when Professor Buchanan made his predictions, the number of cars on Britain's roads has almost doubled. The estimated bill for congestion costs based on calculations of the Road Research Laboratory is in excess of £250 million per annum. Though difficult to calculate precisely, the main costs relate to the impeded movement of vehicles and hence the economic efficiency of the country. Driver frustration and confusing traffic flows with frequent starting and stopping have sent the accident rate soaring. Compensation for personal injury is in the region of £190 million, plus £19 million for damage to and repair of property and £21 million for administrative costs. The Greater London Council has widened pavements and banned cars from the Oxford Street shopping district between Marble Arch and Oxford Circus under an experimental plan to cut accidents, speed the flow of buses, and make conditions better for shoppers. Mr Neil Thorne, chairman of the Greater London Council central area board, was quoted as saying there were more than 300 casualties a year in Oxford Street, thirty times worse than the injury rate on motorways. The scheme is expected to cost £82,000, and savings in running costs to London Transport and in passengers' time should amount to £465,000 a year.

London, the capital and richest city of the nation, has been hardest hit by the new trends: rising car ownership and car usage, declining public transit systems, traffic congestion, changes in daily travel patterns, wholesale destruction of buildings and open spaces by motorways, and the increased isolation and inconvenience of immobilized city dwellers. But whether Londoners like it or not, the car is here to stay. It provides a flexible means of transport and a status symbol for many austerity-weary middle-class people and the better-off sections of the working class. How the car is to be accommodated in the city, however, is an important question, particularly for the non-car-owning public. Three hundred miles of new urban motorway have been proposed by the Greater London Council to ease traffic congestion and to speed the movement of traffic on the periphery. Three concentric rings of motorways will

Table 6

Increase in Number of Motor Vehicles in Britain

Year	All motor vehicles	Cars
1920	650,000	187,000
1930	2,200,000	1,000,000
1939	3,100,000	2,000,000
1950	4,400,000	2,300,000
1960	9,400,000	5,500,000
1970	15,200,000	12,000,000

Source: Tony Aldous, *Battle for the Environment*, London: Fontana, 1972.

move long-distance traffic around the city and improved local street systems will help urban car owners. But there are some doubts about the wisdom of these plans. Two thirds or more of the London population do not have use of a private car. And since the G.L.C. have not published plans for a public transport system which could use the ringways effectively, it seems clear that the minority needs of car drivers are getting priority treatment. The Council's glossy brochures claim that the new roads will cause no great disruption or destruction of good homes, historical buildings, and open spaces. But there is plenty of doubt about this too. Each ringway will probably deprive the city of 1,000 acres of land. And large sections of London's public are up in arms against planners, developers, and road builders. The 'Homes Before Roads' campaign by independent voters in the April 1970 Council elections, though unsuccessful, may gain more powerful public support in the years ahead.

Professor Buchanan, an acknowledged authority in this field, has grave doubts as to whether more motorways would provide a complete answer to congestion and movement problems. In a recent enquiry he reiterated points made in *Traffic in Towns*: 'We believe that there is a need in this country for a vigorous programme of urban road building – not rushed into haphazardly, but as the result of careful analysis of probable traffic flows and needs. But we cannot hold out any hope that this by itself will go very far towards solving the problem.' A comprehensive urban traffic modernization programme is closer to the answer, he suggested, and should be based on creating 'environmental areas' in which the human scale predominates over the use of vehicles, and good environmental standards prevail.

Looked at from another viewpoint, there are many technologists who argue that those who cause congestion can be made to pay and that in time it might be possible to 'price congestion out of existence'. Congestion, they say, is essentially a problem of the disbenefits which follow from the competition of too many vehicles for the same road space. Making congestion a source of government revenue is an intriguing idea, but establishing principles of road pricing, and methods of implementation and disposal of profits is not an easy task. Gabriel Roth, a British engineer-economist, has proposed, in an article in *Traffic Quarterly*, the creation of a city highway authority with a new approach to highway finance. Pricing and investment policies would be based on the following rules. Road users in congested areas impede the movements – and raise the journey time costs – of each other. Hence they would be charged road use costs of not more than one cent per vehicle mile and congestion costs up to $1·20 per vehicle mile. If calculable, environmental costs of noise, fumes, accidents, and loss of amenity to the community at large would also be charged. The authority would pay all costs incurred in providing and maintaining the road system and the interest on loan capital. Profits would be used to expand the service; and limited subsidization would be given to public transport, especially for the young, old, and infirm, and those who cannot afford to own or run cars.

As for the methods of raising revenues, Roth has several suggestions. The main sources of revenue would be congestion taxes augmented by tolls or taxes for the use of the road, fuel and tyre taxes, and annual licence duties on vehicle ownership. Mr Roth defends the view that the provision of roads should be determined by the wishes of the road users through the price mechanism, not by administrative decisions taken at local or national levels.

London's mass transit system is causing concern to the city authorities, especially after shock reports about travelling conditions on the heavily used Northern Line. Meeting mass transit needs is the job of the London Transport Executive, which has responsibility for surface bus transport and the Underground, one of the world's most extensive and busiest rapid transit systems. Both the L.T.E. and British Rail, the major commuter-carrying line, have announced plans to extend their services but are handicapped by financial problems, political inertia, and the competing transport-control powers and plans of the government Department of the Environment and the Greater London Council.

London's commuters and residents received two additional reports in the summer of 1972 which indicated that the transportation picture is gloomy indeed. Mr Horace Cutler, chairman of the Policy and Resources Committee that controls London Transport, revealed in July that the estimated costs for the first stage of the new Fleet Line on London's Underground system had increased in two years from £35 million to £52·9 million. London Transport's 'inaccurate original estimates' were said to be at fault. Hence there is a serious danger of more than a year's delay on the line which will connect transit-poor south London to the Strand, Trafalgar Square, and Baker Street central areas. In June, the G.L.C. and the government were heavily criticized for withholding approval of British Rail's decision to sell off and develop its huge property assets to meet its financial losses, estimated at more than £30 million in 1972. British Rail spokesmen claim that its plum sites in London and the provinces have a development potential of £600–£700 million which within ten years could be bringing in £50 million a year to help the ailing, bankrupt railways. (Its 300 acres of sites in London would also be capable of providing housing for 30,000–50,000 people.)

The whole urban transport system needs to be looked at afresh, says Professor Buchanan, and he gave some hints as to how this might be done before a House of Commons public expenditure subcommittee investigating urban transport planning.

There is need, said Professor Buchanan, for a systematic and comprehensive approach which would review the results of current policies about public and private transport. Ways must be found of weaning car owners away from using their cars for journeys to work and enticing them back to public transport. Every effort should be made to keep the balance of private and public transport by controlling central area parking and improving suburban rail services. The effects of road pricing on land uses must be examined. Studies are also needed of the way in which increased car ownership and usage affects the growth of out-of-town shopping centres and hurts town centre development. Here Professor Buchanan was undoubtedly expressing his fear of the American 'Retail Revolution': the explosive combination of the automobile, suburbanization, high levels of disposable incomes, and the acceptance of once-a-week shopping expeditions which helped the spread of huge hyper-markets and out-of-town shopping.

Tokyo's streets, at the height of the 1960s' boom, had to deal with more than a million cars. This figure was four times the 1955 car population and may double again by 1975. Tokyo authorities won't be able to solve traffic congestion without destroying thousands of acres of housing to build roads. For unlike some Western cities, Paris and Berlin, for example, which have one quarter to two thirds of the city space given over to roads, Tokyo has only 10 per cent. And if the number of car owners using vehicles for work trips increases as is expected, then even the expressways and suburban road networks now being built will be swamped. Commuter congestion on private and national rail systems and at transfer points with municipal subways, trams, and buses is also a problem. And furthermore, the city's extensive underground and surface railway system, which was coping with 1 million passengers a day in 1967, may have to handle 5 million passengers a day before too long.

In Italy the rapid rise in the number of automobiles on the road poses a major problem. In 1960 Italy had 2·5 million cars; by 1970 there were more than 10 million. Average densities of cars per square mile are higher than those in America; and in the next ten years, at present rates, Rome will have enough cars to cover every square foot of road surface. City traffic jams occur four times a day because urban Italians still go home for lunch. Automobile fumes are at dangerous levels and car manufacturers are not required to install emission-control systems. In early 1971, the sulphur dioxide reading in Milan reached more than two parts per million – in London in 1952 a level of 1·34 p.p.m. caused 4,000 deaths. Suffocation and paralysis of the centre of the Renaissance city of Bologna has forced the Communist-controlled council to take drastic steps against the private car. The number of car-owning Bolognese has grown in the decade 1960–70 from one in sixteen to one in three, almost equal to the American figure. At first fourteen miles of roads will be banned to cars and open only to buses and taxis. Public transport will be free. One-way streets will make it hard to cross the city by car and force motorists to use the ring roads. New car parks will be set up around the city with frequent free bus connections to the centre. Professor Renato Zangheri, the mayor, has said that he is prepared to close the entire centre of the city to traffic if these measures don't work.

In the Rhine–Ruhr district, the old road and rail networks don't fit the growth of new urban and industrial developments. The road system laid down in the eighteenth century to serve market towns cannot handle the heavy traffic of a modern polycentric industrial region. Railways built in the late 1800s, primarily for freight and long-distance passengers, are not adequate for the modern commuter. And there is a great need for north–south road and rail links to serve the congested cities of the core and towns in the new development zones. Until recently trams and buses served as good mass transit systems, but now they require overhaul and extension if they are to provide adequate services between new residential and industrial areas.

Moscow planners are relying heavily on traffic controls and mass transit improvements to deal with their problems of movement and congestion. Street-widening schemes and im-proved electronically controlled signals are being introduced at main crossroads. The relatively low car ownership rates will be maintained while emphasis is placed on the electrification and extension of the Métro rapid transit service.

In Paris the new generation of affluent car owners is flooding streets designed in the pre-automobile age of one hundred or more years ago. Spacious tree-lined boulevards designed by Baron Haussmann during the reign of Napoleon the Third were not built to allow kerbside parking. The traffic circles upon which they converge like spokes in a wheel cannot cope with the avalanche of daily traffic. Traffic police have to face daily wrangles with frustrated, wildly gesticulating motorists and with shopkeepers who depend on the scarce kerbside space for deliveries and customer parking. Major congestion also occurs at junctions where road traffic into and out of the city at peak hours clashes with traffic and pedestrians at main line termini, Métro underground stations, and bus transfer points.

Parisian planners accept the fact that car ownership will grow over the next decades and are building a major radial and circular road system to cope with future traffic. New suburban circular roads will move traffic around the city while an inner ring system and east–west motorway will allow penetration into the city centre. There is some fear that this 'motorization' will destroy the unique character of Paris. Hence improvements are being made in the Métro and a deep-level Métro line will be extended to the outer residential and industrial suburbs.

European cities are facing traffic congestion problems on a scale never known before. One of the major causes has been the spectacular growth in the domestic car market. Today there are sixteen large European companies producing 300 different models and 7 million cars annually. (By contrast, in America, four makers supply ninety models and 10 million cars annually.) The top six car makers are Volkswagen, Fiat, Renault, British Leyland, Ford Germany, and Citroën. Car purchases have increased tenfold since 1950 and more motorists are using their cars for convenient door-to-door travel. Road traffic is growing at 5–10 per cent per annum. And at the same time, the haphazard growth of cities and road junctions makes driving a tiring, frustrating nightmare of twists and turns through a maze of narrow streets and 'alternate routes'.

European governments and administrators, like their counterparts in America, have undertaken huge highway-building programmes to relieve the glut on the roads. In France, for example, the once-proud road system inherited from Napoleon and the Third Republic has long since proved inadequate. French motorists, the most highly taxed in Europe, curse the traffic jams and have forced the government to mount a major road-building campaign. Belgium and the Netherlands, in the north of Europe, have built motorways to feed traffic to and from their industrial ports. Germany has constructed 2,756 miles of Autobahns equipped with 190 petrol stations, 150 restaurants and cafeterias, fifty hotels, and other amenities. Italian roadmakers, among the most brilliant highway engineers in the world, have built twenty-five autostrade to deal with the local and inter-city traffic. The most famous long-distance motorway, Autostrada del Sole, runs the 469 miles from Milan to Naples through 113 tunnels and across 572 flyovers. Now all European nations are committed to

Table 7

Europe's Motorways

Country	Miles of motorway		Total operational mileage	Planned mileage
	Per 1000 sq. miles	Per million inhabitants		
Netherlands	43	44	575	1,850 (1985)
W. Germany	29	45	2,756	8,050 (1985)
Belgium	25	31	355	1,100 (1985)
Italy	19	44	2,428	4,150 (1975)
Switzerland	12	31	194	1,100 (1985)
Austria	9	41	306	1,150 (1985)
Britain	8	13	1,000	2,250 (1982)
France	5	19	956	1,850 (1975)
Sweden	2	33	261	950 (1985)

Source: *Union Routière de France* and *The Times*, 7 March 1972 (supplement).

a gigantic and elaborate network of international and trans-continental highways, called E-routes. The completed network will connect Palermo to London via Rome and Paris, and Lisbon to Helsinki via Madrid, Bern, and Stockholm. The E-routes will become, like the railroads before them, a major factor in transforming travel and transport movements and affecting the countryside, suburbs, and central cities.

This European road-building craze is associated with a momentous postwar decline in rail transport. Most rail systems are nationalized and are incurring huge financial losses. The British losses are in excess of £30 million. The French and German systems lose considerably more. The new money-spinner is air travel, rising at a 12 per cent rate of growth and destined to exceed 20 million passengers per year. Since the 1960s, 'the New Europeans' have taken to the air with great enthusiasm. Now more than sixty airlines ply the airways, and when supersonic planes like the Concorde and the big jumbo jets with their 500-passenger payloads come on the scene, airport services will be swamped. As air traffic increases, so do delays – delays getting to and from airports, and delays before take-off with as many as eighty multi-engined planes waiting with their engines running. A normal journey of say one hour, when combined with terminal and landing delays, may add up to a total trip time of six hours. Airports are also voracious space-eaters. Take-off distances are increasing as larger planes are introduced, as are space demands for servicing, loading, and taxi-ing, and parking lots for passengers, visitors, and staff. Large airports also sterilize huge tracts of land in metropolitan areas and make it almost impossible to live or farm in adjacent areas. It is now abundantly clear that these new rail and air transport problems will require immediate attention within the framework of national and European community economic development.

The American Case

America is in an advanced state of traffic congestion and of the transportation crisis. Car numbers grew by 50 per cent in the last ten years. Half of all vehicle miles are driven in cities on streets and roads which are heavily congested. The car dominates the major cities. At least two thirds of all daily work trips are made by car, and only 20 per cent are made by public transit. Los Angeles is of course the most often quoted example of this pattern. But in fact eight American cities exceed the Los Angeles level of car usage, and in the top five – Houston, Cincinnati, Kansas City, Dallas, and San Antonio – automobiles carry more than 70 per cent of all those riding into the heart of town.

Automobiles also play a key role in inter-city travel. Eighty-six per cent of all travel between cities and half of all trips of more than 1,000 miles are made by car. Annual travel statistics per capita by car have leapt from a total of 2,400 miles in 1940 to 7,000 in 1970. In doing so the motor car has completely altered city and inter-city travel patterns and become the country's cheapest form of transportation. In the meantime, railroads lost $10 billion on lost passenger mileage, which makes them the most uneconomic transport activity in the country's history.

The major indictment against the car is cost – in economic and social terms. The car costs the country billions of dollars a year more than the $93·5 billion people are spending to buy, fuel, clean, insure, repair, park, and provide roads for it. It accounts for at least half the pollution bill of $11 billion. Automobile accidents not covered by insurance cost about $6 billion a year, and free parking on streets represents an additional subsidy of several billions of dollars to car owners.

The private automobile is least efficient by capacity, by pollution produced per passenger mile, and in use of capital invested. In many high-density cities, cars carry well under 10 per cent of commuters but cause at least 70 per cent of the traffic jams. Cars also are inefficient in terms of land use. In downtown areas they together take up too much space to deliver too few persons to their destinations. Buses, taxis, trains, and even bicycles could do the job better – if some drastic changes were made.

At the present moment, however, the owner and user costs per mile by car, when two or more persons are riding, are cheaper than public transport – and more convenient. The fatal mistake has been to sacrifice other forms of transport to the private car. It is becoming absolutely clear that greater balance is needed between the car and other modes of urban transportation. The key sector for change is that of the commercial services like taxis, local buses, mass transit, and inter-city buses and trains – which represent a mere 5 per cent of all expenditures on passenger transport at present. This $5 billion sector, small and shrinking as it is, contains part of the solution to the problems of traffic congestion and the transportation crisis.

In the United States only 20 per cent of all work trips are made by public transit. This varies widely from 2 per cent in smaller cities, to around 67 per cent in New York City. The proportion is between 33 and 50 per cent in cities like Chicago, Boston, Washington, New Orleans, and Philadelphia. Generally the cities with well-developed transit systems have a low percentage of car owners driving to work. Rail commutation is only a small fraction of all daily work trips by mass transportation and is concentrated in a few cities; for example, roughly one third of all rail commuting in America takes place in the New York City region.

Transit riding has steadily declined since 1950. Passengers on streetcars decreased by 78 per cent, buses by 28 per cent, and subway and elevated rapid transit by 17 per cent. Today the average American uses public transit half as frequently as in the 1920s, and spends less money on fares. Over the same period the annual average expenditures on automobile transportation, particularly for driving in cities, rose dramatically.

Faced with the dominance of the car, there has been a rush to accommodate it on the nation's roads and highways. The Bureau of Public Roads argues that new expressways will speed traffic around and through the cities, and will relieve downtown traffic congestion. The new federally-aided Highway Act, partially subsidized by motor vehicle owners to the tune of $25 billion in federal taxes, will finance over the next decade the completion of a 41,000-mile Interstate super-highway system criss-crossing America. When the final 10,500 miles are finished, a motorist will be able to make the coast-to-coast trip in forty-eight hours, about half the time it takes at present.

In some places the new Interstate highway will be a vast and beautiful scenic parkway. But along the connecting beltways and at interchange points in urban areas, the Interstate has brought with it a sterile look-alike monotony of filling stations, motels, shopping centres, and apartment blocks. The completed sections have already had crucial effects both inside and outside of cities. The Interstate has bisected urban areas, bypassed and caused the decline of farm towns, and opened up rural areas to developers and speculators. The Interstate has encouraged the shift of labour markets, populations and retail stores, warehouses and factories into the suburbs. Businesses have thrived or shrivelled, and whole industries have been transformed. In the Midwest, small-town packing houses are now linked by fast highways to major markets. This has administered the *coup de grâce* to the monopolies formerly held by big-city slaughterhouses and meat-packing industries in Chicago, Kansas City, and Omaha. Railroads, urban transit systems, and feeder airlines have also been affected. Road truckers have captured over 70 per cent of the nation's total freight revenues. Automobiles have taken off with the former rail passenger. Today a businessman can fly to the big city nearest his small-town destination and with a drive-it-yourself rented car double or triple the market he can reach in a few hours.

Bull-dozing its way into cities, the Interstate highway brings with it long-term and widespread effects. The central district has been transformed from a mixed residential, retailing, and manufacturing hub to a financial office and business centre surrounded by expanding rings of slums and suburbs beyond. Retail stores have shifted to the beltways and the suburbs. Millions of new car commuters have been created by providing the primary linkages on the periphery between expanding suburban retail, residential, and industrial centres. Amenity areas and recreational facilities have been swamped. Highway contractors and landowners and speculators have made millions. Auto-rental companies have expanded and doubled their revenues in ten years. Hotel industries have grown; for example, there are now 545 Holiday motor inns situated at key interchanges of the system, and the chain grossed more than $1·2 billion in 1970.

The negative effects of the Interstate highway system did not pass without criticism from urban taxpayers, public bodies, and municipal officials, and by the mid-1960s an active opposition movement began. Lawsuits and injunctions by angry local residents and city officials brought construction work to a halt in fifteen cities – Boston, Chicago, Hartford, Providence, Philadelphia, New York, Baltimore, Washington, Memphis, Nashville, Shreveport, Cleveland, San Antonio, San Francisco, and Seattle.

The major complaints were against noise and air pollution from heavy traffic, and the disruption of neighbourhoods and community linkages. In the Washington, D.C., area there was a bitter legal battle over the merits and demerits of the Three Sisters Bridge connecting the Virginia suburbs. Lower Manhattanites fought against an eight-lane expressway. Black neighbourhoods in Washington brought lawsuits against plans to demolish their homes for highway construction. Planners, students, and middle-class protest groups stopped road construction in metropolitan Boston and on the Inner Beltway through Cambridge. There were protests against a six-lane road through the historic Vieux Carré quarter of New Orleans. And a national highway action

81

coalition was organized to press for reforms at all levels of government.

Counter movements have been formed by powerful national associations of automobile owners, manufacturers, truckers, and road builders. They opened large Washington offices and spent more than $100 million a year wooing support for highway construction among power elites – congressmen, senators, and senior members of the armed forces. One of the most powerful organizations is the American Association of State Highway Officials. Its members are responsible for laying out the routes of the nation's roads, selecting designs, and letting contracts. Their view is that highway construction should proceed at all costs, with or without the support of a 'few dissident groups'. At the height of the controversy Mr Alfred Johnson, executive director of the association, was quoted in a *Fortune* magazine special report on transportation as saying, 'We've got about 235 miles of Interstate which are causing all the trouble, most of them in cities. As far as I'm concerned we should just forget them. If people don't want the highways to come into town, then we can increase the capacity of the beltways to bypass them.' But this won't be easy to put into practice for the simple reason that the road sections in urban areas carry the heaviest traffic and hence generate a proportionately heavy share of the highway taxes that pay for the system's construction.

Faced with this tense situation, there has been a noticeable growth of opposition to highway building coming from the White House and the Department of Transportation. Even the National Conference of Governors and the National Conference of Mayors have been obliged to acknowledge opposition spokesmen. After fifteen years and $43 billion spent on its construction, the Interstate highway system has met some of its transport and military objectives; it has improved road travel between cities and provided a base for coping with future traffic growth in less built-up areas. But it has clearly failed to correct urban congestion, one of its principal objectives. The beltways encircling major cities have created severe land-use problems. They are heavily congested with local traffic, particularly near interchanges, and have generated the need for more roads farther outside the city to carry through traffic.

The Interstate controversy sparked off new investigative and experimental programmes on the national and state level. On a broad national front, the U.S. Department of Housing and Urban Development (H.U.D.) proposed a $980-million grant programme in urban transportation in the fields of research, demonstration projects, and training and technical studies. (The first Secretary of H.U.D. is George Romney, ex-president of American Motors and the Automobile Manufacturers' Association, and former Governor of Michigan.) H.U.D.'s goals are laid down in the report *Tomorrow's Transportation – New Systems for the Urban Future*. They are to evaluate and forecast the impacts of transportation planning as an integral part of comprehensive urban development. Modernized transportation systems, says the H.U.D. report, are part of the general objectives of metropolitan societies: efficient use of resources and increased accessibility to greater opportunity. They can contribute to the urban future in four main ways: (1) offering a range of choice and diversity; (2) enabling development of a stronger 'sense of community'; (3) giving equitable access to jobs and education through links with industrial growth centres in and around cities; and (4) enabling accessibility through road pricing systems, improved travel time, and rational urban layout and design.

Closely allied with H.U.D.'s activities is the Department of Transportation, whose first Secretary was John A. Volpe, three-time Governor of Massachusetts, a wealthy director of a highway construction company, former Federal Highway Administrator, and 'architect' of the Interstate Highway Program. The Department serves as a model for the work of more than thirteen state transportation departments. Some of the solutions currently under investigation include improving existing arterial roads, reserving lanes on express roads for buses, and differential parking fees to encourage the use of car pools. There are also studies of how taxation measures can force the motorist out of his car and on to public transportation for the final leg of his daily commuting journey.

Some states are considering ways to utilize highway revenues to finance bus transport systems, particularly reserved bus lanes, fringe parking areas, bus turnabouts, passenger shelters, and off-street parking lots. The belief is that these devices coupled with modern equipment and scientific route designs can put buses back in the mass transport picture and reduce peak-hour automobile traffic congestion.

Little of this experimental activity will change the dominant fact that consumer choice in America is heavily weighted in favour of the automobile. And what is the more grave and disturbing fact is that a very large section of urban America – the poor and low-income families – is more seriously disadvantaged now than ever before. Given the trends towards scatteration and sprawl, declining transportation systems, and increasing car ownership, a heavy burden is placed on the shoulders of unskilled breadwinners of the urban poor and low-income families. In central cities almost one in every three households is without a car, and since many of them are poor they are almost entirely dependent on public transit. They are deprived of access in an automotive civilization to a range of metropolitan job opportunities because they are either carless, isolated, or ill-served by transportation at fares within their means. This situation raises many important questions about the need to establish a minimum standard of mobility in an affluent society.

Let's start with the car and see what the situation is. One half of all American households own one car, another quarter have two or more cars. For well-to-do car owners, access to jobs and urban facilities is improving. On the other hand, 20 per cent of American households do not own cars. They are the Transit Dependents – the low-income poor, the old, the handicapped, and youth under twenty years of age – and the trends are against them. Even the low-income families who own cars – and half of them do – are in a bind because their vehicles are nine or ten years old, dilapidated, and unsuitable for continuous daily use on new expressways.

Clearly the major expressway projects proposed for metropolitan areas stand little chance of aiding immobilized transit dependents. In fact, they serve the needs of the suburban middle classes rather than the inner-city poor. Suburban car-owning families have access both to decentralized employment and shopping activities, and to basic urban services and activities, thanks to the new motorway craze. As a result, suburban families, unlike the inner-city poor, do not have to trade off accessibility for savings in location rent, they can have both. Given increasing ease of movement along expressways, living in suburbia becomes the most rational residential choice for middle-class families.

Buses do not help the inner-city poor very much either. Time losses are an important deterrent, and car users in general win again. Bus riders travelling in the same direction as the main-stream of traffic spend about twice as much time going between the same two points as car users. Time losses obviously mean losses in potential income and, as bus riders get exasperated with bus services, they will acquire and use cars and abandon bus systems, except for downtown journeys where parking is too

Table 8

Automobile Ownership by Income Group, U.S.A., 1966

	Percentage distribution of spending units by ownership of automobiles		
	Owns 1	Owns 2 or more	Owns none
All spending units	54%	25%	21%
Money income before taxes (1965)			
Under $1,000	21	3	76
1,000–1,999	28	3	69
2,000–2,999	51	3	46
3,000–3,999	61	6	33
4,000–4,999	65	11	24
5,000–5,999	68	16	16
6,000–7,499	68	21	11
7,500–9,999	63	30	7
10,000–14,999	50	46	4
15,000 and over	35	60	5

A spending unit consists of all persons living in the same dwelling and related by blood, marriage, or adoption, who pool their income for major items of expenses. Some families contain two or more spending units.

Source: Survey of Consumer Finances, conducted by the Survey Research Center of the University of Michigan.

expensive. Thus low-density bus routes serving the non-central business district will become less used. As ridership drops, routes will be discontinued and those who most depend on buses will become more isolated.

Mass transit subways present difficulties for the poor also. The trouble is that public transit does not start where they want to start or go where they have to go. Transit systems are downtown-oriented and the expanding job centres are in the suburbs. Central-area low-income slum dwellers have to travel farther to workplaces than other urban dwellers. In one of New York's black ghettos, the Bedford-Stuyvesant area of Brooklyn, three quarters of the labour force work outside Manhattan. By comparison, only half the city's labour force show this characteristic. These differences reflect the decreasing significance of Manhattan as an employment centre for low-skilled and unskilled labour. Part of the cause is the decentralization of manufacturing into the outer boroughs and surrounding counties of the New York area. How to match up jobs and workplaces becomes therefore a major problem.

In New York City, new land-use changes have emphasized the cruel mismatch of jobs, homes, and mass transit. The booming central-city economy focuses on white-collar and skilled blue-collar employment. Manufacturing and low-skill industries are joining new industries in the outer reaches. All the evidence presently at hand points in the direction of this shift. In the last two decades, 195 new office buildings in a few square miles of midtown and downtown Manhattan have added 67 million square feet of office space – twice the total office space available in the next nine largest U.S. cities combined – and 50 million more square feet are under construction or on the drawing board. This massive change in land use has displaced and scattered inner-city jobs and homes to other areas of the city, and has had a tremendous impact on existing residential enclaves.

New York City's people live in fairly distinct enclaves of obsolescence and opportunity according to class, ethnic, and racial backgrounds. Large areas of the oldest inner-city housing exist in East Harlem and Harlem, South Bronx–Morrisania, Bedford-Stuyvesant, and South Jamaica. They are congested slums, and largely black and Puerto Rican quarters. White working-class immigrant minorities – Irish, Italian, and Jewish families – live in the industrial and port areas of Hunts Point in the Bronx, Long Island City and Maspeth in Queens, Greenpoint, Williamsburg, South Brooklyn, Red Hook, and Gowanus in Brooklyn. Middle-class white neighbourhoods can be found in high-density apartment blocks and terraced housing in Manhattan, Queens, Brooklyn, and the Bronx, and in the 1920–30 outer suburbs. These outer suburbs, though badly served at present by sewerage and transit links, are areas of attraction and new settlement for inner-city working-class whites and new industries.

New York City's Planning Commission has published a large-scale plan for extending mass transit to the outlying areas so that their residents will be able to get into their central-city jobs quickly and efficiently. Meanwhile the poor and deprived inner-city residents are faced with no jobs in the centre and a lack of adequate links with suburban job centres. A million and a half of the jobs in New York pay less than a man needs to support a family even if he works full time. More often than not the jobs are seasonal with long periods of unemployment. They are dead-end jobs, and most low-paid workers cannot get better jobs because they do not have the education or the training. They are the high school drop-outs, the semi-literate migrants, or the people whose skills are outdated or irrelevant. Though the majority of low-paid workers are whites, the hardest hit are the younger low-skilled blacks and Puerto Ricans.

Paradoxically, in the case of rapid transit systems as well as highways, the major beneficiaries are middle-income suburbanites who still work in the city. Newly proposed mass transit systems in San Francisco, Oakland, New York City, and Washington, D.C., will speed suburbanites into and out of the city but will do very little to help give increased mobility to the poor. For example, while 57 per cent of the white middle-class residents of Montgomery County, Maryland (the richest county in America), with jobs in Washington are expected to use the new subway, it will serve only 21 per cent of the Washington residents employed in Montgomery County. Thus the new $2·5 billion Washington transit system will not be a major factor in carrying minority groups to the suburbs. The same is true in regard to the BART system, designed to serve the San Francisco–Oakland area, and the projected billion-dollar expansion of the New York City subway system.

In America today the public services are inadequate and unequal as far as the urban poor are concerned and unrelated to even the best intentions of those who preach about enabling access to opportunity. Harvey Perloff, a former professor of planning at the University of Chicago, commented on this recently. 'Transportation planning in our metropolitan regions,' he said, 'has rarely been closely related to the various community economic development programmes – the programmes seeking to affect new industries.' Nor, says Perloff, 'has it provided a continuing interplay between decisions about where to locate workplaces, homes and transportation links'. Even rarer, he noted, are attempts to link transportation decisions to anti-poverty programmes when it is obvious that transportation is an important element in any effort to minimize unemployment and poverty.

The facts are that urban growth and change inhibit deprived and increasingly transit-dependent unskilled job seekers from access to a full range of metropolitan job opportunities. More knowledge is needed. What is the link between transport deprivation and unemployment? What is the potential value of subsidizing rapid transit systems as an instrument of an anti-poverty policy? What kinds of transit subsidies do the most good? How much do they cost per worker helped? What proportion of the unemployed can be helped by transit subsidies alone, or within a wider programme of social welfare? These are questions that government, industry, planners, and the middle classes have to answer.

There is no shortage of new ideas for moving urban dwellers around the city; for example, taxi-bus systems. One type is the Dial-a-Bus, a cross between a bus and a taxi. You just call and state your destination and a computer using a mathematical routing formula picks the appropriate bus and sends it to you. Customers may have to wait a bit longer and the bus does take a more circuitous route, but the novel Dial-a-Bus system is reckoned to be a cheaper form of urban transport. So much so that planners of Milton Keynes, a British new town, are proposing to install a Dial-a-Bus system for the use of its 250,000 inhabitants. Another is the Jitney bus, a form of runabout transport common in America in the 1920s and still flourishing in many of the underdeveloped regions of the world. Jitney buses are generally cars or estate wagons bearing destination cards which ply the city streets looking for passengers. They operate like buses and stick to fixed routes, run on a schedule of sorts, and charge a sliding scale of fees. Mass transport planners in America are considering introducing Jitney buses in poor city areas.

Taxi-bus systems have a number of merits in their favour. They provide a variety of one-person and multi-passenger services. This service flexibility also allows for pricing flexibility, which is very important for the poor. By charging lower fares for trips which either begin or end in a poverty zone, the poor may be subsidized by wealthier riders of the system.

American proponents of the taxi-bus say that it can do what other systems do not do – go where the demand is and only when the demand is ready to be satisfied. It can give faster service than a taxi at about one-fourth its cost, roughly 15 cents per mile. This may be of particular significance to the low-income poor, for in many places more poor people use taxis than do rich people.

For long trips, the taxi-bus system can act as a feeder and distributor to a mass transit vehicle. For example, on a trip to a plant in the suburbs, the taxi-bus might pick up a person in the city and take him a mile to an express bus stop where he begins a five-mile express ride, at the end of which he might transfer to another taxi-bus for a $1\frac{1}{2}$-mile trip to the plant. The per-mile cost of the whole trip might be as low as $8\frac{1}{2}$ cents, which compares with the cost per mile of a Volkswagen. And on an annual cost basis, it represents about one half that of owning a Volkswagen.

Some of the current anti-poverty palliatives proposed range from issuing discount credit cards which allow free or low-cost travel for trips beginning and ending in poverty areas to loans for purchasing new low-cost small cars, like the Volkswagen and the Austin Mini. According to one proposal put forward in the *Traffic Quarterly* by Sumner Myers for personal transportation for the poor, a 'cars-for-jobs programme could give low-income wage earners and the unemployed a stake in society and motivate the poor'. Myers estimates that a new Volkswagen can deliver 7,500 miles per year of highly reliable transportation for about the same annual cost as a nine-year-old jalopy. A subsidy programme could be organized to help with discount purchases and loans for the car and all operating costs. A central organization could be responsible for obtaining tax exemption grants, credit card purchases of gas and oil, and the collection of receipts for submission to tax authorities for refunds. The new car would be in effect a subsidy for people who are actively looking for better jobs, and could be linked with the efforts of an employment referral service. The central organization could be responsible for three additional functions. It could arrange for the resale of cars, say, after 25,000 miles, and organize a car-pool clearing house requiring clients to pick up and deliver anybody going in the same direction. It could also fit the cars with speed-control and monitoring devices to encourage safe driving. Used cars could be provided under similar conditions, and the organization could also instruct low-income workers in consumer education, car maintenance, and mechanics.

Myers's attempt to solve the transport problems of the poor by making them car owners and drivers, though quite novel in many ways, seems about as myopic as Marie Antoinette's suggestion to the hungry French masses: 'Let them eat cake.' It neatly welds the elite poor to the auto-culture and gives them a debt which they will have to work hard to pay off. It puts more cars on the road and hence exacerbates problems associated with the car in cities. It clearly does not help those who do not or cannot drive. In addition, the Volkswagen Myers admires so much has been condemned as 'dangerous and accident prone' by Ralph Nader and other militant defenders of America's consumers.

'Free transit for better job mobility' is another palliative proposed to help the job-seeking poor. But a recent study in Boston by Gerald Kraft and Thomas Domencich came to the opposite conclusion. Free transit cannot help poorer workers get access to better jobs simply because there is a mismatch between poverty areas and low-skill job centres. The connecting transport links are just not there. Furthermore, the cost of providing expanded transit services between poverty areas and low-skill job centres would be only 6 per cent of the estimated annual costs of providing 'free transit' service for the Boston area. Why, ask the authors, should the city council endorse the larger expenditure on free transit to achieve the lesser gain of transit mobility for the poor? Their view is that more effort should be given to making present systems work better and service the public and the poor more economically.

America's urban transportation crisis is crucial to the lives of millions of urban poor whites, blacks, Puerto Ricans, Mexicans, and other deprived minorities. Transport is part of their struggle for social validity, for access to the material and cultural resource delivery system. They live in the oldest housing areas, and face patterns of *de facto* segregation which keep them in ghettos and out of the suburbs. They suffer from high rates of unemployment, welfare dependency, social pathology, and an opportunity loss in all areas of urban life. They have witnessed the failure of fragmented urban renewal programmes, and the punitive use of public housing to pen them in isolated places outside the mainstream of American life. They have also seen how rapid transit systems confer most benefits upon upper-income groups and bypass their own needs. Better, cheaper, and new forms of transport may provide some solutions. But they are not the sole answer to the problems of the poor. For them, and for beleaguered central-city populations in many world cities, the first order of business is the abolition of unemployment, the raising of incomes, the elimination of racial, class, and religious discrimination, and the general improvement of municipal and social services.

The 'Anti-City'

In all the world's major cities, transportation systems are approaching breaking point. They are either bankrupt like most commuter railroads, dangerous to life, limb, and the environment like automobiles, or discriminatory against the poor in fares and services as are many bus and subway lines.

Mass transit systems created in the early twentieth century – the subway, tram, bus, and rail routes – are out of phase with the emerging patterns of today. The dominance of central-city workplaces as focal points for short, twice-daily journeys by public transit from densely packed working-class residential areas, and long-distance commuting by rail from low-density middle-class suburbs, is being challenged. Urban growth and change has scattered homes, workplaces, and recreation areas around the city and significantly altered travel patterns. More city-dwelling service workers are travelling from the city at off-peak hours to jobs in suburban factories, offices, and construction sites. A far greater number of persons is also commuting across the city between low-density residential areas and workplaces dotted around the city. And as the volume of these new travel patterns increases, traditional mass transit systems are finding it harder to cope.

At the same time the quality of service on public rapid transit has declined. Every day millions of city dwellers travel at peak hours on overloaded and outmoded transit systems. People have to walk excessive distances to and from stations. They complain about scores of major and minor daily irritations: poor connections and transfers, infrequent service, unreliability, slow speed and delays, crowding, noise, lack of comfort, and inadequate public information. Urban transit systems suffer from obsolescence and rigidity. A great deal of transit and rail mileage is bankrupt, and much of the rest is deteriorating physically and financially. Management and implementation procedures are outmoded. Too many new transportation programmes are crudely designed and there is a marked lack of public participation in transportation planning.

The car – one symbol of the metallic power of the twentieth century – is choking cities, destroying townscapes, and laying waste the countryside. Heavy traffic in towns has clogged the arteries of surface movement and slowly eaten away at the central-city heart of metropolitan areas. Motor vehicles on roads and in parking lots eat up space. Interchanges and rights-of-way require expensive amounts of land and compete with other important uses of land resources. In older American cities, for example, motor vehicles command about 20 per cent of central-area land; but in the western and more modern American cities which grew up with the automobile, the percentage soars considerably.

Every new car on the road adds another debit to the huge bill of social costs the public has to pay: congestion, pollution, and losses in time, money, life, and limb. The car is killing off people at the rate of a medium-sized war. More than ten times as many Americans were killed in road accidents during the 1960s as were killed in the Viet Nam War. In the United Kingdom, three quarters of all accidents are in the urban areas, and according to Professor Colin Buchanan's survey *Traffic in Towns*, road deaths are ten to forty times as high as those among workers in the most hazardous industries, mines, and farming enterprises.

The debris of motorized societies also takes its toll. Hazards arise on roads from abandoned cars and the crumpled hulks of smashed vehicles, from spillage of bulk materials and dangerous chemicals, and from the litter of tourists and careless drivers. Major accidents at key traffic junctions tie the rest of the city up in knots and require platoons of ambulances, emergency crews, and squads of policemen to untangle the confusion. It is highly probable that future generations will be appalled at the thought of the rivers of death that run outside our doors today. The untamed motorist and his metallic steed will seem as strange and primitive to them as the thought of seventeenth-century surgical operations without anaesthetics does to us now.

Congestion at the centre is accompanied by scatteration and sprawl at the periphery of cities. The automobile has exploded the metropolis wide open and no amount of public transport will jam it back together again. The automobile looks like an unbeatable innovation for circulating people from low-density communities to low-density activities of all kinds. It can therefore be expected that every new road project completed will entice more motorists on the road, increase congestion, waste more land, and consume more public and household finances.

The decline of public transportation and the dominance of the motor vehicle in modern auto-cultures has brought tremendous benefits to powerful interests and pressure groups. The major beneficiaries are the big companies which produce the raw materials, like cement and asbestos, the motor vehicles, accessories, and components. The road haulage and transport industries benefit also, as do road builders and service industries like garages, motels, automobile and tourist clubs. Fortunes have been made by unscrupulous politicians, property developers, and speculators in land-use activities like drive-in cinemas, banks, and shopping centres. But the losers are the majority of non-car-owning, transit-riding public. And in addition there is a growing inequality of access to transport and to urban opportunity that immobilizes and isolates the carless poor and deprived families, the very young, the old and handicapped, and secondary workers in one-car families.

The city is the worse for these changes as well. The major culprits are the six 'false friends of the city', as Victor Gruen, a planner, calls them in *Who Designs America?*, edited by Laurence B. Holland. One is *the traffickist*, who 'lives and dies for the "facilitation" of automobile traffic, and accordingly is engaged in an unholy crusade, willing to bring to his goddess, the Automotive Vehicle, a supreme sacrifice, the city and all its inhabitants'. Another is *the bulldozerite*, who 'is hell-bent on demolition, and starts to think about the replacement of buildings, communities, and urban values only after the damage has been done'. *The paver*, a third 'false friend', is part of a small clique of construction bosses whose tentacles reach even into the Mafia. 'His dream', says Gruen, is to pave the entire U.S. with concrete and asphalt. He envisions a nation buried under six-lane, limited access turnpikes. When the last blade of American grass is buried, he plans to go on to pave Europe. Then Asia. And on and on until the whole planet is coated in cement. Today America – tomorrow the world – we must move cars.

The segregator, another false friend, is a simple, methodical, myopic soul who plans communities on the basis of statistics, land-use maps, and cost yardsticks – but is devoid of any concern for the human dimension of planning and of the intricate and sensitive relations between community, landscape, and topography. In the central city, he creates civic areas, cultural centres, and gilded ghettos separated from other life-giving urban activities. In the suburbs, he produces huge sterile housing areas in which everybody must drive long distances to shopping, work, and leisure centres.

The projectite has a fixation for large complexes of architectural monotony, all constructed at the same time and inhabited by people of similar economic and cultural backgrounds. 'Projectitis' is encouraged by a distorted view of building economics, i.e. repeating the same building forms over and over to reduce construction costs and enhance the profits of builders.

Finally there is *the economizer*, a conservative, pessimistic employee or consultant of government, real estate, or building concerns. In place of a brain he has an adding machine, which he uses to eliminate every ounce of imagination in building designs and layouts on the grounds that 'it costs too much'.

These false friends of the city, says Gruen, in tandem with other forces of modern technology and urban sprawl, are leading to the 'anti-city', a huge, scattered, centreless, sprawling motopia that is a caricature of the city and civilization. A place where, as Gertrude Stein might say, 'there is no there there'.

As Lewis Mumford had predicted years before, the solution has become the problem. In order to overcome the fatal stagnation of traffic in and around cities, highway engineers and planners create remedies that actually expand the evils they are meant to cure. The clover-leaf junctions, the multi-level interchanges and expressways butcher the urban landscape in exactly the same way as the railroad's freight and marshalling yards did almost a century ago. They destroy natural routes of circulation, create clots of intense congestion, and sterilize vast acres of land. Furthermore, the new highways tempt people who have been using public transport to take their cars for downtown journeys. Cities become more congested. Finally all the business and industry that originally gave rise to the congestion leave the city to escape suffocation, leaving a waste of expressways and parking lots in their wake. In the end, all that is left is 'a tomb of concrete covering the dead corpse of the city'.

Considerations of cost and space, environmental concern, and public opinion all argue against undertaking new systems of urban expressways. The challenge is to cope with increased flows of people and goods without more building – to make more efficient use of existing highways and to strengthen public transportation. It is no longer sufficient to examine highway proposals solely in terms of traffic service, economics, and engineering feasibility. New considerations must be given to the social and environmental impact of highways. In urban regions attention must be focused on using highways as arteries for mass transportation, and on fresh concepts concerned with moving people rather than with moving vehicles. Urban transportation must be seen as part of a total movement system, whose constituent parts are planned and financed in a co-ordinated manner, and not as a series of unrelated modes whose end result is clogged cities, inaccessible airports, bankrupt railroads, and the poverty of immobility.

4　Pollution and the Environment

Urban pollution is an inevitable by-product of the city: its burgeoning populations, their extravagant profit-making, waste-producing, and energy-using activities, and the pious hopes of municipal authorities and industrial executives that more technological medicine will solve deep-rooted societal sicknesses. Pollution, plainly defined, is a state of severe contamination of the natural and man-made environment which inhibits a desired use and threatens human health. It is caused by the overloading of the environment with pollutants, the noxious substances contained in our daily industrial, household, and agricultural wastes: garbage, poisonous fluids and gases, noise, heat and energy, detergents, fertilizers, and pesticides. These pollutants are the by-products of 'throw-away' economies and affluent urban societies – the things we have made, used, and thrown away. Discarded heedlessly in the air, land, and water, they become 'the wrong thing, in the wrong place, at the wrong time'. The result is a vandalized atmosphere and landscape – city skies filled with smog, streets littered with waste and eco-pornography, rivers that blaze, and lakes that suffocate and die a slow, smelly death.

Urban Pollution

The central areas of world cities – with their huge daytime populations, jammed streets, frustrated commuters and office workers, shoppers and motorists, intense sales and media competition, sudden surges and halts of traffic, and their industry, building, and construction works – all generate huge waste and pollution problems. The result is stress on human beings and municipal services alike.

Consider the air pollution problems of New York City dwellers. In the summer of 1970, Mayor Lindsay had to decide whether to permit Consolidated Edison, the monopoly supplier of electricity, to build a new power station. If the plant is not built, said Consolidated Edison, there will not be enough power to run the city's traffic controls, subways, and television sets, and supply electricity for all the other needs. On the other hand if it is built, said anti-pollution groups, more sulphurous fumes will pour into the already polluted atmosphere and may be responsible for countless more cases of lung diseases and even death. It was widely recognized, in addition, that any alternative type of power station, nuclear or hydro-electric, would take too long to build and would probably pollute the city's water instead of the air. There seemed no reasonable way out of the problem. For even if 'Clean Air' campaigns are successful and New York is prevented from getting dirtier, chaos might result from electricity shortages. Colour television sets will show grey pictures, computerized communication and control systems will go haywire, jeopardizing banking systems and traffic, and elevators and subways will grind to a halt. And if thousands of commuters switch over to using their cars to get to work in Manhattan, they will pollute the air with more deadly petrol fumes.

In eastern America, during one extremely bad pollution episode in 1971, a stagnant air mass hung persistently over most of the 'Bos-Wash' megalopolis. The situation was so bad that a federal court judge ordered the closing of twenty-three smoke-belching factories. Measurements showed that Manhattan was getting only one third of the sunshine that it should have been receiving. The other two thirds was blocked out by dirty air. With the tops of Manhattan's skyscrapers smudged in a brown murky mass, conditions approached the point where a 'Stage One' air pollution alert might be required. Motorists were asked to leave their cars at home. City officials went on twenty-four-hour standby duty in readiness for emergency action if the situation worsened.

Persistent day-to-day exposure to air pollution has far-reaching effects. Doctors in Los Angeles, where smog fills the atmosphere seven out of every sixteen days, have urged residents who have no compelling reason to remain to move out of the area because 'smog cripples and kills'. Despite all efforts, there has been no improvement in air quality in the Los Angeles basin. Pollution from nitrogen oxides has soared, largely because manufacturers have increased the compression ratios of automobile engines. Hydrocarbon and carbon monoxide levels have remained high. And the future does not look any brighter. More people using more automobiles to travel between home and jobs, plus the resistance of industry and townships to smog control, combine to militate against a successful air pollution abatement and control programme.

Rome's Tiber River is an open sewer receiving all the wastes of the city's 3 million residents at the rate of twenty cubic metres a second. But this is only one third of the filth that goes into the Tiber; the rest is from the effluents of numerous light industries. The condition of waterways in or near other cities is no better. Most wastes – human and industrial – are simply dumped into local rivers. Eighty per cent of Italy's coastal cities have no sewage treatment facilities. City-generated industrial, residential, and leisure activities pollute shorelines, and the vinyl bags in which Italians wrap their garbage litter the land and the once lovely beaches. 'There is not the slightest evidence of conscience or concern for the future,' laments the conservationist Antonio Cederna. 'Industries act like the cat who hides its own dirt with its paws' and 'every protest suffocates against the mattress of political inertia'. Slowly, the courts and regional governments are beginning to stir. Gianfranco Amendola, a Rome magistrate, has spearheaded a crusade to 'bring back life to the Tiber' by fining 400 firms 600,000 lire (£400) each for polluting the river. Conservation groups like Italia Nostra, based in Rome, have prodded the government into curbing urban sprawl and commercial development in parks and special amenity areas. And Dr Aurelio Peccei, a board member of two giant companies, Olivetti and Fiat, founded the Conservationist Club of Rome to persuade governments, industrial leaders, and trade unionists to face the facts of pollution.

London's Thames and its tributaries serve the city as a means of navigation, supply, amenity, and recreation, and as a convenient waste-disposal unit. Civic and governmental action in the last fifteen years has greatly improved its condition, but rarely does the water moving sluggishly through the central area have more than 5 per cent of its maximum oxygen content. The amount of organic matter, chlorides, nitrates, and phosphates in the water has increased considerably, and with it has come an increase in water costs because of the higher cost of water treatment.

London's traffic, according to a special report on noise, is the predominant source of public annoyance. Central London has the biggest noise problem, exceeded only by noise levels on motorways and at airports. Regularly seventy and eighty ear-deadening decibels are registered as heavy traffic grinds through cramped streets. Without costly extensive double glazing, sound insulation, road screening, and reversal of building fronts from roads, it will be very difficult to cut out noise from London's vast number of older houses and commercial properties.

Aircraft noise is a growing problem. In the flight paths leading to and from Heathrow Airport, noise is regularly recorded at the level of 115 decibels. Noise-reduction measures have been tried, for example a system of preferential runways and special night-flying restrictions, but with little success. The British Airports Authority is offering financial inducements, such as cheaper landing fees, to airlines that reduce noise. But such proposals are unlikely to influence the wealthier airlines, which have the larger aircraft, operate the most flights, and also make the most noise.

Clean air laws and smokeless fuels introduced in the late 1950s brought remarkable improvements in London's air quality. So did the Clean Air Act of 1968. But they did not legislate against sulphur dioxide, and a new crisis is at hand. Visible pollution has been cut down, but fumes, grit, and acid are still unleashed into the air at an alarming rate. Studies by the British Medical Research Council have confirmed a positive correlation between sulphur oxide pollution and infections of the lower respiratory tract; and bronchitis-emphysema, a pollution-linked respiratory disease, is the leading cause of death among males over forty-five years of age. Now with the rising use of oil fuels for central heating, industrial energy, and motor vehicles new dangerous airborne pollutants – polycyclic hydrocarbons, carbon monoxide, nitrogen oxides, lead, and vanadium – have been added to the traditional ones of sulphur dioxide.

These grim findings, when seen in the context of London's fog-prone climate, have caused renewed fears of another smog disaster – a lethal mass of sulphurous smoke and fog. Sulphur oxides and soot are the key elements of the problem. When combined with fog they have played a murderous role in public health annals. In 1952, during a foggy, severely cold December weekend, the smoke fumes from coal-burning home fires and factories hovered over London. Levels of sulphur dioxide in the air rose to twice the usual level. Smog reduced visibility down to three feet. Cinema patrons could barely see the screen. People inadvertently walked off the Thames River banks into the cold waters. An aeroplane pilot trying to taxi to a terminal at Heathrow Airport after an instrument landing got lost; so did the search party sent to find him. Several prize cattle on display at the Smithfield Livestock Show perished. And the consensus was that 4,000 human lives were snuffed out by the death-dealing smog. Ten years later, again in December, 700 deaths due to smog were recorded. No one knows when the next disaster may strike, and worse yet, few people seem to care enough to introduce effective safeguards to public health.

Twenty-five years of wild economic and population growth have left Tokyo choking for breath. Now that there is a pause in Japan's reckless race for economic development, municipal authorities are wondering what to do about the city's massive pollution problems and environmental disaster areas.

Tokyo harbour is clogged with industrial effluents from factories, port activities, and power stations, and with the sewage and refuse from millions of households. Despite the metropolitan government's declared aim of abolishing crude methods of sewage disposal and installing an urban drainage system, progress is slow and the city now faces a critical sewage pollution problem – critical because of the risk of contamination of water supply and marine life upon which the Japanese depend for food.

Tokyo's refuse collection and disposal system is a massive chaotic enterprise. The city's garbage trucks are squat, fast, noisy, and painted royal blue and their drivers, the *gomi-tora*, are notoriously the most ruthless and reckless in all Japan. Every twenty-four hours they collect 13,400 tons of rubbish from the twenty-three central-city districts. A third of it is burned and the rest is hustled at the rate of 5,200 trips a day through the narrow residential streets of Koto-cho ward, just east of the Stock Exchange, to the docks. And from there it is transported to a stinking, rat-ridden, man-made island just offshore in Tokyo's harbour which rejoices in the name of Shin-Yumi-no-Shima – 'New Dream Island'.

Residents along the garbage-strewn path to the docks have protested at this intolerable assault on their environment and have sent delegations of housewives and teachers to see Tokyo's Socialist governor, Ryokichi Minobe. In reply Minobe offered to solve the problem by substituting three-ton trucks for the present one-ton trucks, thereby reducing the number of journeys by 1,000; banning island dumping; and building alternative disposal plants. But these goals will not be easy to implement. The three-ton trucks will cause more problems than they solve. They are too big for Tokyo's narrow winding streets, and any attempt at road widening will mean purchasing huge amounts of land exorbitantly priced at £42 per square foot, and the displacement of thousands of families, thereby intensifying the existing housing shortage. The unwieldy trucks will cause huge traffic jams and increase air pollution dangers, particularly from Tokyo's speciality – photo-chemical smog – which turns cabbages white and has sent schools full of children home choking.

The artificial islands, foul as they may be, are part of Tokyo's elaborate and vital land-reclamation programme. Any cutback in their development would be a blow to the hopes of many thousands of slum dwellers for better housing. As regards building new disposal plants, seven of them are proposed for the suburbs by 1975, but in every one of the suburbs there is a well-organized local opposition movement. No one wants to import the problems of Koto-cho ward. In suburban Suginami ward, Minobe has promised to build an underground access road to the plant costing £1 million, but at that price garbage incineration becomes excessively expensive.

Photographs taken by satellite show that Tokyo has a massive air pollution problem, more grave even than London or Los Angeles. And according to the 1971 Pollution White Paper, Tokyo has the most lethal atmosphere in all Japan. Industry is the main polluter and the main target for pollution control. In the mid-1960s university students approached municipal authorities with a proposal for limiting factory production each week to cut down emissions into the atmosphere. They argued that economic growth was sufficiently high to absorb a voluntary cut in industrial activity. The plan was rejected with the explanation that 'things will have to get a lot worse before they get better'.

And they *have* got worse. In July 1970, smoke, fog, and exhaust fumes were trapped over the city for a week. Schools were abandoned, anti-smog masks were normal wearing apparel, and street-corner oxygen vending machines did a booming business.

In the face of these problems, the Japanese have shown a remarkable ingenuity in creating palliatives – environmental placebos which like many doctors' pills do neither harm, nor any good. 'No Car Days' are popular, and in a western Tokyo neighbourhood 'No Smoking' and 'No Garbage' days were held during which housewives were shown how to cook with minimum waste. Aichi Prefecture, which includes the big industrial cities of Nagoya and Chita, held a 'Blue Sky Day'. At 9.00 a.m. one morning all firms and factories were asked to reduce smoke by 20 per cent and at midday by 50 per cent. Measurements of sulphur dioxide, dust, and carbon monoxide were recorded to be used against the worst offenders.

The anti-pollution engineering business is also booming. Every oil company executive and chemical plant builder is praising the value of his own super-exclusive sulphur-extraction process. According to the Japan Development Bank, something like 7 per cent of all capital spending by Japanese industry in the fiscal year 1971 was devoted directly or specifically to the control of various kinds of pollution – a figure that is nevertheless a mere drop in the bucket in a country so short of sanitary facilities and municipal social services. One company, Kawasaki Steel in the Tokyo–Yokohama area, has sought to ease its ecological conscience by establishing fairly stringent control mechanisms. The contract for its new £150-million No. 4 blast furnace forbids any production to start until a vast range of specified controls has been installed and is working. And as soon as air or water pollution reaches rigidly set limits in the area, the entire plant must be shut down.

But despite these individual actions, the old problems remain. In the massively industrialized Tokyo–Chiba strip, where steel works, oil refineries, and petro-chemical plants jostle each other for eighteen smog-ridden miles, one is proudly told that new housing development is forbidden in the area. But the fate of the existing residents in the great blocks of workers' flats along the main road is unchanged. 'They were built under the old regulations,' say company managers, and their inhabitants are doomed to continue to live with the world's highest evidence of respiratory disorders.

The large mass of workers and citizens are not able to cope with these problems. Health, welfare, and disability schemes are still quite primitive and an old age pensioner's monthly allowance is as little as £2.50. It is cold comfort to them to know that any sufferer of asthma or bronchitis-emphysema can get automatic compensation from a special £1·25 million Air Pollution Victims Fund, or for their children to know that teachers are promised premium pay and quicker promotion if they agree to work in 'high pollution zones'.

Moscow presents many interesting contrasts to other world cities: such as its inland location, its monocentric urban base, and its socialist political system and objectives. 'Moscow is not the graveyard of a forgotten civilization,' said *Izvestia* in 1925, 'but the cradle of a new growing proletarian culture based on labour and knowledge. These are the great principles that guided the revolution, which must also be reflected in the external visible aspects of our way of life, in our taste, in our works, in our style, and in our architecture.'

Upon first view, Moscow exhibits a dramatic representation of Russia's politico-economic philosophies. Public litter and refuse dumping are negligible problems, mainly because there is less emphasis on production for consumer goods and more emphasis on prolonging the life of products. Moscow has efficient street-cleaning and refuse-collection services, and there is a social stigma attached to being a 'litter bug'. Commercial detergents are rarely used in households and hence pollution from this source is non-existent.

Moscow has fewer air pollution problems from transport and motor vehicles than one would expect in a city of its size. There is an extensive and efficient underground and surface public transport system, and electric trolley buses. Far fewer motor vehicles are privately owned; well-subscribed car hire and taxi-pool services are available; and considerably less ethyl lead is added to motor fuels. As a result, Muscovites breathe air with a significantly less polluted content than that found in most large cities in the West. Ordinary street noise levels are low, and as far as aircraft noise is concerned, the two major airports at Vnukovo and Sheremetyevo and the new airport at Domodedovo are located away from the built-up area of Moscow and its satellites.

Air pollution from domestic sources is also lower in Moscow, despite cold winters, because of the use of steam district heating provided by a publicly owned enterprise called Telovaia Elektro-tsentral (TET). TET supplies heat and hot water to entire neighbourhoods in most Russian cities. It is estimated that 50 per cent of all heat consumption is provided centrally in the Soviet Union, and two thirds of this is supplied by a network of

TET stations. This makes possible, say heating engineers, a hotter fire, better smoke control, and therefore a more efficient form of combustion and less air pollution.

But in a nation whose productive drive has thrust it into the top industrial nations of the world and whose capital city accounts for a large share of that production, the problems of air pollution from the mills of development loom as large as they do in all the world's great cities. Most of Moscow's major industries are ill-equipped to curb emissions of smoke, grit, and soot. Only recently has the Moscow City Council, according to Chief Architect Mikhail Posokhin, moved to enforce effectively measures to equip factories with dust catchers and cinder traps, and to propose improvements in the control of emission of fumes, vapours, and gases.

In the case of water pollution, industry and municipalities are the major culprits. Sewage treatment facilities are inadequate and a large proportion of Moscow's industries discharge their untreated effluent directly into the environment. Many other cities and suburbs in the most advanced of all soviet republics, the Russian Soviet Federated Socialist Republic, are hopelessly behind even these modest standards. Two thirds of all housing units in urban areas are not served by a sewage system and a similar proportion of the cities and suburbs have no equipment for treating their sewage.

Pollution Spreads

Pollution is not a new problem. Far from it. Man has been polluting his environment ever since he entered into it. But the rapid rise of pollution up the list of highly dangerous urban problems is due to the changing character of human activities and settlements. In the historical past, so long as human numbers were small, the effects of man's activities could be absorbed and dissipated naturally. At each stage of rapid growth in human settlements and their productive capacity, however, the threat to man and his environment has increased in quantum jumps.

In Middle Eastern towns of the Neolithic Age, like Çatal Hüyük and Jericho, pollution was due mainly to human wastes deposited on land, residues from small tanneries, copper-working, and pottery industries entering water and soil systems, and smoke from wood and dung fires. Pollution rose dramatically with the coming of the Industrial Revolution. By the early nineteenth century, coal was the main fuel. It fired the steam engines that pumped water from mines, worked bellows, and drove iron hammers and machinery. Coal-burning, tall-chimneyed mills and the huge encampments of densely packed grimy houses around them threw up a pall of sulphurous smoke and cast their wastes upon 'green and pleasant land' and into open drains and ditches. It was the age of the 'triumph of industry and the glory of man'. But in the mill towns and cities there were open sores of filth and disease. Household refuse and human waste accumulated in the crowded courts and alleys until putrefied, sold, and carted away to the fields by the muck-shifters.

Within their homes and workplaces, the working classes lived lives of utter degradation, and this aspect was unrelieved outside their deprived confines. The young Communist and cotton merchant Friedrich Engels in his book *The Condition of the Working Class in England* (1844–5) called the River Irk in Manchester

a narrow, coal black foul smelling stream full of debris and refuse which it deposits on the shallow right bank. In dry weather, a long string of the most disgusting blackish green slime pools are left standing on the bank, from the depths of which bubbles of miasmatic gas constantly arise and give forth a stench unendurable even on the bridge forty or fifty feet above the surface of the stream.

Twentieth-century urban industrial societies are polluters *par excellence*. They produce more dense populations, more goods, and hence more pollutants, waste, and dereliction than the world has ever known. Every item manufactured, packaged, and sold produces waste in the form of solids, liquids, and gases. These waste products are disposed of into the air, land, and water by the cheapest means available. As a result the environment within and around cities becomes a huge receptacle for the offal of urban industrial societies.

The 'Energy Society', so proudly proclaimed by Americans, is itself a major polluter which holds urban man in a vise between recurring black-outs and brown-outs and the environmental consequences of increased energy production. Businessmen and industrialists who profit from the sale of electricity and electric appliances push more and more 'convenience products' on gullible consumers. Massive advertising campaigns urge consumers to make their homes 'all electric'; to install colour television and no-frost refrigerators – which in fact use more electricity than conventional appliances – to put air conditioners in every room, and to 'make life easier' with electric-powered toothbrushes, blenders, cutlery, and shoe-shine machines. The result of increased industrial and consumer demand for energy production to run mills, machines, and appliances is more disfigurement of the landscape by power plants and high-voltage transmission lines, more thermal pollution of surface waters used for cooling generators, and more air pollution by heat, sulphur oxides, and particulate matter thrown off from fuels used by electricity generating stations.

In America, toxic matter is being released into the air at a rate of about 200 million tons a year, or nearly a ton for every American. It comes from 90 million motor vehicles, from factories, mills and refineries, power plants, municipal dumps, homes, and back-yard incinerators. And there is every indication that tomorrow's air pollution levels will be even higher. By the year 2000, the U.S. population will be almost double what it was in 1960. These people will drive cars, manufacture goods, heat buildings, use electrical power in much the same way as today. By 2000 most major industries, including those that create pollution, will have increased production, the number of cars may have quadrupled and will burn 160 billion gallons of gasoline each year. The need for electrical power will be about six times greater. And the estimated 280 million urban dwellers concentrated in cities will bear the brunt of the air-pollution problem.

The worst noise problems in the urban environment affect the 130 million Americans now living in metropolitan areas. More people are exposed to the all-pervasive continuous hum of vehicular traffic. Over 7 million workers are exposed to noise levels that may damage their hearing over a prolonged period of time. Communities around major airports, for example the heavily used O'Hare Field in Chicago, Kennedy Airport in New York, and the International Airport at Los Angeles, get heavy intermittent doses of outdoor noise exposure.

Americans throw away 360 million tons of household, municipal, and industrial solid wastes per day. Waste disposal is a costly enterprise. On a nationwide basis the total expenditure for collection of trash and other solid waste by public and private concerns is approximately $4·5 billion per year. Household waste amounts to 190 million tons per year or 5·3 pounds per person per day. By 1980, the amount collected by similar means is expected to be over 340 million tons per year or eight pounds per person per day. Most disposal systems are inefficient and contribute to land and water pollution.

Many urban water treatment plants are hopelessly outmoded, overloaded, and inadequately staffed. Most water-works operators are low-grade, low-paid employees who lack formal training in treatment processes, disinfection, micro-biology, and chemistry. Within the next fifty years, according to some forecasts, the demand for water by cities will grow considerably and the water pollution rates may double. This will place great pressure on available water supplies and more intervention will be required just to keep things from getting worse. More water will have to be re-used, and it will cost more to retrieve clean water from progressively dirtier waterways.

In all the world's great cities the effects of urban pollution have spread into the surrounding countryside. The city region is the pollution fall-out zone. It is there that one finds great chunks of wasteland, the drab oppressive vistas of filling stations, light industry, housing development, the vegetation deadened by sulphuric acid, rivers killed by poisonous fluids, and hideous cemeteries for the abandoned, wrecked, worn-out hulks of the machine age.

And farther afield still, urban pollution extends over very large regions. Smoke and stench clouds formed in industrial New Jersey choke New York City; and those formed in Texas cities appear 1,000 miles away in Cincinnati, Ohio. Air pollutants from Britain and Germany account for one third of Sweden's atmospheric pollution. The wastes of oil ports and industrial cities in Europe pollute harbours, estuaries, and the coastal waters of the English Channel, the North Sea, the Baltic, and the Mediterranean. Thor Heyerdahl, the intrepid oceanic sailor, found gross signs of refuse dumping in the Atlantic Ocean. One lone occupant of a deserted small island in the Inner Hebrides counted no fewer than 149 non-bio-degradable objects manufactured in England, America, Germany, and Russia, washed up on the sand and pebble beaches. These included at least fifty plastic bottles, several sheets of polythene, a Wellington boot, a hub-cap, a nylon broom head, and the body of a disposable hypodermic syringe.

Urban man's impact on the environment is a national and supra-national crisis. Scandinavia, once the world's symbol of orderly bourgeois democratic affluence, now finds itself swamped with wastes. Norway's fjords are awash with stinking cakes of solid wastes, and Sweden's pine copses are redolent with the litter and garbage of weekend leisure-hungry crowds. Infections picked up at polluted beaches near Rome have sent typhoid fever and hepatitis soaring to near-epidemic proportions. The Rhine, that great European sewer, picks up 15 million cubic yards of waste yearly en route to Holland, which the Dutch have cynically dubbed 'the rubbish bin of the world'.

Cleaning up the muck of urban industrial economies adds billions to the waste bills of modern nations. The American waste bill, estimated at $4·5 billion per year, includes the costs of cleaning up the effects of 20 million tons of paper, 48 billion cans, 26 billion bottles and jars, 3 billion tons of waste rock and mill tailings, and 50 trillion gallons of hot water. Aggregate costs of air, water, and solid waste pollution control may well exceed these figures. Richard Revelle, Professor of Population Policy Studies at Harvard University, estimates that the annual costs of pollution control in American cities over the next fifteen years, for both capital and operating costs, would be $13·5 billion. In Sweden, a country with one of the highest standards of living in Europe, the cost of cleaning up the natural environment over the next decade is expected to be $3 billion or about 10 per cent of the Swedish gross national product. Swedish planners and administrators may have to deal with an atmospheric load of 1·5 million tons of sulphuric acid, especially over conurbations; 450 million tons of waste water emptied into lakes and waterways; 2·5 million tons of garbage; 300 million non-returnable glass bottles chucked away in meadows, woods, and forests; and 140,000 wrecked cars abandoned in otherwise idyllic birch woods and pine copses.

What Is Being Done?

Popular anxiety about urban pollution is an economic and political factor that no administration can afford to ignore, especially after the startling mobilization of public opinion and environmental action groups during the late 1960s. Conflicts of interest between people and conflicts about short-term and long-term objectives make urban pollution and environmental improvement intensely controversial subjects. In some countries, like America, they are already a major domestic issue; in others, local citizens are rapidly making their views known.

London's conservationists have applauded the government's proposals for a comprehensive approach to urban and environmental problems. It created the world's first Department of the Environment, at full ministerial level, which consolidates traditional areas of concern, like land uses, housing, transport, research, and planning, with new powers and resources to provide a total approach to environmental problems. Peter Walker, the first Secretary of State for the Environment, called for a ban on supersonic flights over Britain, more money for Clean Air and Smokeless Zones, and for sewage disposal, stricter control over vehicle noise and exhausts, and a 'spill now pay later' law that will make oil pollution more expensive to tanker owners. From now on, he said, 'whoever causes pollution must either be prevented from doing so, or pay the cost of clearing it up'.

But all is not well on the environmental front in Britain. Making the polluter pay only leads to higher prices, said one environmental writer, Miss Jacky Gillot, in *The Times* 'Letters to the Editor' column. Another campaigner for environmental improvement, Professor Peter Self of the London School of Economics and Vice-Chairman of the Executive Committee of the influential Town and Country Planning Association, observed that 'what is required is a shift of the whole economy from policies encouraging more stress to those encouraging less stress on the environment. Policies based on assumptions of maximum consumption, limitless growth, rapid turnover, activity rates, increases in GNP, physical mobility and alleged economies of scale should be ended.' In their place, he concluded, emphasis should be given to policies encouraging greater intrinsic satisfaction of work, durable artefacts, concern for the quality of the environment, the balanced community, and the devolution of government from the centre to the public.

In Tokyo, environmental action groups backed by middle-class conservationists have mounted their attack on many pollution fronts. The daily newspapers are filled with 'environmental victories'. At Christmas and New Year department stores are urged to curtail their passion for elaborate gift wrapping. Mass pressure is put on large companies by the victims of effluent disposal malpractices. There is a multi-million-dollar government fund to soundproof schools, hospitals, and homes, and to pay half the television licence fee in areas suffering from aircraft noise. Some Osaka residents have sued for $250,000 in 'compensation for sleep'. And the Tokyo Patent Office is deluged daily with schemes for plastics that rot in the sun and machines that turn old tyres into building materials.

New legislation is in the offing as a result of pressures from more than 250 civic associations prepared to form a Citizens Federation Against Nuisances. An Environmental Agency was created in July 1971, and its director, Boichi Oishi, has ministerial rank. Top priorities on his list of tasks, say conservationists, should be saving the only decent beach at Yokohama, scheduled to be rebuilt an industrial estate as part of the government's land reclamation programme, protecting rare plants threatened by a big highway across Honsu Marshes, and dealing with oil pollution of coastal areas.

But will the efforts of the environmentalists choke off the great engine of national prosperity? Or will they merely switch the national energy into newer, healthier, and even more prosperous industrially exploitable fields? Tokyo certainly does not know. One day in the winter when the skies were a beautiful and totally unaccustomed blue, a member of the Stock Exchange was heard to say, 'Ah, recession weather . . . you only see blue skies when the oil refineries are not burning.' And even the brokers are no longer really sure whether they want the blue skies or the smoke.

Los Angeles citizens' groups and planners have called for a formidable array of anti-pollution control techniques and strategies for a 'war against smog'. These include a co-ordinated research programme, a new Air Pollution Control Department, legal sanctions against motorists whose cars emit excessive exhaust fumes, and smog control legislation affecting industry and homes. Planners in the Rhine–Ruhr urban region have experimented with green strips of vegetation and trees between major settlements against the prevailing winds to encourage dispersal of air pollutants. Other planners are at work on the problems of the River Emscher, which crosses the core area of the Ruhr and empties into the Rhine River. The Emscher supplies a great deal of water for washing vast quantities of Ruhr hard coal, some 80 per cent of Germany's output, and consequently is laden with dust. Now through an intricate and costly recycling process, most of the polluted water is treated before it reaches the Rhine, and the salvaged dust is used to supply 90 per cent of the fuel requirements for local power stations.

Metropolitan authorities affected by new forms of waterborne wastes are contemplating installation of water treatment facilities that remove more subtle pollutants. Though advanced facilities are rare in the United States, a 7,500,000-gallon-per-day plant at Lake Tahoe, California, is providing an interesting model for use in metropolitan areas. The Tahoe installation is notable in that it removes both first-stage sludge deposits or heavy particles from the waste water and the remaining organic matter, and then removes both phosphate and nitrogen, the undesirable nutrients which cause proliferation of algae. When the effluent is finally passed through activated carbon, the product is almost good enough to drink.

Ironically, this advanced technique intensifies one of the most pressing operational problems in waste-water treatment. Namely, how to dispose of the sludge, the solid matter removed from domestic and industrial waste water. Sludge is a nuisance and highly contaminable unless it is thoroughly disinfected. Its disposal, like waste disposal in general, costs money and can consume half the budget of a treatment plant. Furthermore, when communities dry and burn their sludge, it pollutes the air. Finally, though last-stage cleansing with chemicals produces cleaner water, the result is even greater quantities of sludge.

Chicago presents an example of some of the difficulties and perhaps an effective way of coping with sludge, for a while longer. With 1,000 tons of sludge a day to dispose of, the Metropolitan sanitary district has been stuffing about half of it into deep holes near treatment plants, at a cost of about $60 per ton. The other half is dried and shipped to Florida and elsewhere, where it is sold to citrus growers and agri-business companies using fertilizers for $12 per ton, a non-profit-making operation. Mr Vinton W. Bacon, General Superintendent of the sanitary district, says that this state of affairs cannot continue. 'We are running out of land. Not only that, but the land we are using for disposal is valuable and even it will be filled within two years.'

European nations have taken up the challenge of urban pollution and environmental problems and are approaching them on a number of different levels. A World Conference of Public Participation in the Fight Against Pollution was held in Sofia, Bulgaria, in April 1972. The French Centre of Urban Research created a new portfolio of urban and environmental studies, and the government appointed a Minister of the Environment directly responsible to the Prime Minister.

For most of Europe's technocrats, however, the problem is not the salvation of cities but the systematic exploitation of the economic problems underlying pollution problems. For example, the Organization for Economic Co-operation and Development and NATO, the military–political union between America and European powers, are co-ordinating urban anti-pollution control with economic development. Eight large projects are underway to reconstruct polluting urban systems in European cities. An American-sponsored project is using two cities in Germany and Turkey as measuring points of air pollution. One is Frankfurt, a high-density industrial area; the other is Ankara, situated in a valley whose atmosphere is badly polluted by burning high-sulphur-content lignite coal. Mathematical diffusion models will be used to set standards of acceptable levels of pollution and to predict climatic events twenty years hence.

Scientists at OECD research institutes in major cities are tackling anti-pollution and economic development programmes from another angle – the re-use or substitution of fossil fuels. They recognize that 60 per cent of all pollution is from the combustion of fossil fuels for industrial and residential purposes. Based on statistics of energy use in cities and regions, they have proposed a range of technical options with far-reaching implications for European cities and economies. Choices could be made to (1) change the energy source; for example, from oil to nuclear power, or to a type of fossil fuel containing less of the pollutants; (2) process the fuel for the specific purpose of removing pollutants; for example, converting coal to either gas or liquid form to reduce the sulphur content; (3) increase the efficiency of the combustion process so that it leaves fewer by-products; (4) change the type of combustion; (5) provide better thermal insulation for buildings and encourage the use of central heating; and (6) remove the impurities after combustion. Evaluating these alternatives will not be an easy task. New technological knowledge is necessary, particularly in regard to control devices for nitrogen particulates. Further information is needed about how costs vary in relation to different fuel sources, the opportunities for non-urban siting, the potential of new combustion and generating techniques, and the types of waste removal and recycling techniques required. And at the end of the exercise, the final decision about acceptability will be a political one made by governments.

On balance, it would seem true that pollution and pollution control in urban societies directly or ultimately relate to issues of profit and advantage – economics and politics – whether for government, industry, or consumers, though these issues are often masked in technocratic or humanistic phrases.

In capitalist societies, under the present set of rules, if one enterprise is a good environmental citizen, incurring heavy debts in the fight against pollution, and if its competitor operates on the principle of the 'environment-be-damned', then the first enterprise will be punished and the second rewarded. The market practises selection against the environment. Correction of the market is very difficult in that growing class of situations where the negative effects on the environment do not occur until the product is in the hands of the consumer and then discarded. Automobiles, convenience foods, packaged goods, and most consumer goods fall into this category – all the things that 'make life worth living'. Still more difficult to deal with is the product that interferes with some method of waste disposal. The polyvinyl chloride bottle really produces problems when it is burned in a trash incinerator equipped with a scrubber designed to catch soot and fly ash. The burning PVC causes hydrochloric acid to form on the scrubber, thereby destroying its metal casing. In future, as new, more esoteric compounds are introduced on to the market, the protection of the environment will require public policies that force innovators to pay more attention to the side effects of their products. The danger, say industrialists in their own defence, is whether stringent public measures will prevent new worthwhile innovations from ever coming into use, or worse still from the consumers' point of view, raise the price of products out of the reach of ordinary people.

There is little doubt that Moscow and other Russian cities caught up in the drive for economic development in the Soviet Union have also produced polluting ethics, polluting economic structures, and problems of urban and environmental pollution not too dissimilar from those in the West. Though the Soviet economy is state-owned and centrally planned, it has proven unable to adjust the cost-accounting system so that each enterprise pays not only its direct costs of production for labour, raw materials, and equipment, but also its social costs of production arising from such by-products as dirty air and water. It also finds it difficult to create clear lines of authority and responsibility for enforcing pollution control regulations. Protests about the growing problems of urban-industrial pollution have appeared in journals like *Izvestia*, *Literaturnaya Gazeta*, *Trud*, and *Krokodil*, but with little effect, and it will probably take a new generation of Soviet citizens to answer questions like: 'Why in a socialist country, whose constitution explicitly says the public interest may not be ignored with impunity, are the executives of industry permitted to break the laws protecting urban life and nature? Can Soviet socialism undertake radical measures to ensure the efficient conservation of nature and the healthy growth of socialist cities?'

Cities Are out of Phase

Appeals to industry, citizens, and city administrators, new anti-pollution technology, more cost-effective measures to protect the environment, stiffer taxation, and stricter enforcement powers have all got to be tried. But it seems clear that even more sensitive and socially responsible initiatives will be of very limited help unless they are accompanied by new rules of the game. Urban pollution is part of the high-technology, high-production problem. It would have been unimaginable 150 years ago that clean air and water could become scarce commodities. These resources were considered common property and used without charge. Since then the price of everything else the economy uses – land, minerals, food, labour, and time – has become dearer. But clean air and water, though now precious, are still left out of the pricing system, still free of charge and unprotected by the state in the name of the common good. Though a manufacturer, or a municipality for that matter, is under great pressure to offset rising labour and material costs by developing new techniques, it is under no comparable pressure with respect to clean air and water. The result puts a heavy load on 'free' resources, and there is a huge market incentive in the pricing system which supports pollution.

The fact is that cities and urbanized societies as we know them today are out of phase with ecological reality. Urban man pollutes his habitat and environment as a function of the way he lives, works, and satisfies his gargantuan everyday needs and desires. Enormous amounts of water, food, and fuel are consumed and wastes discharged in the form of sewage, refuse, and air pollutants. Ordinarily human densities and activities are dealt with by natural cycles of the environment and the help of man's technology, but a crisis comes when, as the population builds up, it contaminates the environment with its own waste products. If this crisis is not solved, death or dispersal of the population is inevitable.

So far man has 'solved' each of the crises with ingenuity, luck, and a belief in his own divine right to survive. But each solution of a crisis carries with it the seeds of a new crisis, because the solutions introduced permit even larger concentrations of populations, with increased needs for survival, and hence greater volumes of pollutants which then demand more drastic solutions.

In the decades immediately ahead, pressures to produce more goods and services will build up tremendously. Industrial and consumer demands will be felt in five crucial markets of change: the markets for shelter, energy and power, food, transport, and communications. This will mean more metals, chemicals, and resources used and cast aside, and hence more grievous assaults on man and his environment.

Urban pollution coupled with runaway production, consumption, and technology place man in a triple bind. They pollute his cities and life-support systems, they subject him to stress and chronic disorders, and they recklessly rob the earth's resources. If disaster is to be avoided, the rate of pollution and misuse of resources must be drastically reduced. These are the sombre conclusions of a remarkable report by Dr Dennis L. Meadows and a group of seventeen scientists at the Massachusetts Institute of Technology, entitled *The Limits to Growth*, and published for the influential environmental action group, the Club of Rome. The main conclusions are incontrovertible, says Dennis Gabor, Professor Emeritus in Applied Electron Physics at the University of London: 'We are on a catastrophic course, and if we do not prepare in time, we shall have to learn from Malthusian catastrophes, on a scale which the world has never experienced in all its history.'

5 Alienation, Conflict, and Violence

Urban man is the litmus paper of this great age of transition. The costs of rapid change are etched upon his social relations, his culture, and his nervous system. The continuous assault on his senses plays havoc with the mind and emotions. The dehumanizing artificiality of unrelieved boredom with possessions negates the image of the city as a place of light, beauty, and reason. City dwelling becomes more and more an absurd and exhausting tragi-comedy. As a result, the price of living in the city is a constant state of anxiety bordering on panic. There is a crisis of human identity in cities, and the illness lies somewhere down in the urbanized society itself, inside its value conflicts, its exploitative social institutions, and its alienated individuals.

City Problems in Perspective

The great metropolitan centres of population and wealth contain, on average, the richest, healthiest, best educated, housed, and serviced people in the world. Their administrative, professional, and business elites pride themselves on being innovators in a quick-reacting, wide-open cultural system, and use the metropolis as a vast staging-ground for the mobilization of manpower and the expansion of productive capital. But each new stage of metropolitan development reveals grave and fundamental structural defects at all levels of society and tremendous problems of alienation and social conflict that grow in virulence with the quickening tempo of change.

New York City is the fabled hub of the East Coast megalopolis, but despite its grandeur and expanding wealth, it has a huge backlog of social problems and rising rates of family disorganization and broken homes, venereal disease, and mental illness. Mass migration, high mobility, and urban renewal have left the city with large areas of slum-shocked families, a lack of elementary social services, and public primary and secondary schools unable to produce students who can take advantage of higher education and job opportunities.

Reports from Italy indicate a similar pattern of culture shock. The growth of job centres and booming cities – Florence, Rome, Naples, Palermo, Milan, Turin, and Bologna – has crushed the life-giving vigour of the old style of life. Italian city culture, once defined by the piazza, the market, the trattoria, the bar, and the church, is doomed to pass into a disruptive modern phase.

In Britain, loss of identity on the national scale is correlated with social schizophrenia on the urban scale. London's adaptation to the decline of British imperial power and her entry into the Common Market requires relearning how to live in the face of uncertainty. And this is painful. The metropolis, which was once the innovator *par excellence*, is now the imitator. And as one observer commented, 'The physical rebuilding of the capital is a painful assemblage of second-hand ideas and palely reflected alien zest. London is not at all sure just what it is the capital of today.' Successive governments have concentrated on revaluing sterling currency, balancing the economy, increasing production, and attaining a competitive position in world markets. But organizing British society for a triumphant and untrammelled entry into the twenty-first century is proving difficult. Student protests and demonstrations at prestigious, elite institutions, strikes by refuse collectors, postmen, and dockers, a rising rate of crime and armed bank robberies, and the smell of scandal in high places all indicate a rift in the social fabric. Today's London and its people are part of the nation's unresolved tensions and dilemmas of choice between continuity and change, elitism and egalitarianism, traditional culture and deliberate, and necessary, social reform.

Japan's Tokyo–Yokohama urban complex epitomizes the tremendous impact of urban industrial growth on the culture of a traditional society. Its past is based on irrigated rice agriculture, familism, unending toil, and fatalism. Interpersonal relations were governed by intricate patterns of etiquette stressing family solidarity, shades of distinction in status and honour, and aesthetic sensitivity to physical objects and human feelings. Its present is a metropolitan vortex of restless striving, personal ambition, property ownership, and the material thrust of an affluent society.

People are deserting the countryside. Most of Japan's forty-six prefectures lost population during the last inter-censal period. The metropolitan region is growing by leaps and bounds – and so are the rates of crime, suicide, family disputes, male–female conflicts, and mental breakdowns.

Recent studies by the Japanese Psychological Association and publications like the *Japan Statistical Yearbook* confirm that Tokyo is a focal point of innovation, secularization, and individualization. Traditional patriarchal social structures, such as the extended family and the paternalistic business or factory, are breaking down. The impact of the city is at a maximum in the market-place and the job, with less dramatic changes occurring as a result of the influence of Christianity, higher divorce rates, and lower death rates. Youth face the challenge of competing to maintain or secure a place in the urban social hierarchy, which roughly divides people into five groups: the political and industrial elite; the bureaucratic 'salarymen'; the small-scale artisans and storekeepers; the new masses of urban factory workers; and the poor country people. Education is the mechanism for selecting and training individuals for their roles in the hierarchy. Competitive stress in late adolescence at the transition point from high school to university or first job takes its toll. Newspapers are filled with tragic stories of youthful suicides. For example one young man, despondent over his failure to pass a college entrance examination, committed suicide by electrocuting himself on a high-tension wire. In his pocket was a scribbled note saying he felt he could no longer live in this world because he was 'too weak-minded'. The intense concentration of pressure during the brief period of adolescence is related to a most unusual fact about suicide in Japan. It is the one country where the suicide rate is extremely high in the late teens and early twenties and declines sharply between thirty and fifty years of age.

In all the world's great cities deep fissures have appeared in the urban social system – the interconnected sets of values and activities that define the boundaries of orderly existence. The welter of problems we see in them are not strange and unpredictable maladies, however; they are stark reflections of the social costs of adaptation to city life in changing urbanized societies.

Alienation

Urban society fragments the individual into compartmentalized roles and thwarts the creation of socially responsive citizens. Highly competitive striving for achievement and social status leads to pathological fears of failure and rejection. Boring repetitive jobs, justified on the grounds of efficiency and profit, force workers to become more adroit and less industrious. And under these circumstances, in the same proportion that the worker improves his work production, the person is degraded. Middle-class workers are no freer from alienation. They are 'cheerful robots', as the sociologist C. Wright Mills points out in *White Collar*:

In many strata of white-collar employment, such traits as courtesy, helpfulness, and kindness, once intimate, are now part of the impersonal means of livelihood. Self-alienation is thus an accompaniment of ... alienated labour ... When white-collar people get jobs they sell not only their time and energy but their personalities as well.

Urban culture produces its own brand of illness. The psychic climate induces nervous tensions, sudden heart seizures, and chronic mental illness – a fact confirmed again by the mid-Manhattan survey, an authoritative large-scale report by Professor Leo Srole of the distribution of symptoms in an urban population. Frequent emotional upset and mental distress are 'central city' afflictions, especially among the poor and deprived and among 'status-movers' up and down the socioeconomic scale. Many anxiety-ridden urban dwellers suffering from real or imagined psycho-physiological disorders are seduced by the media and by the medical and pharmaceutical industries into feeding their neuroses with a colossal daily intake of pills, depressants, health foods, vitamins, calories, tobacco, alcohol, and drugs.

Urban man seems prone to a state of mind that Emile Durkheim, one of the founders of modern sociology, described as 'anomie'. It is a typical response when the norms of social life – the rules of the game – appear inapplicable, contradictory, or no longer relevant to the achievement of one's goals. A general loss of social orientation follows, accompanied by feelings of emptiness and apathy. It is a state of 'normlessness' in which 'life has no meaning'. Three human desires are uniquely frustrated in the metropolis: the desires for community, engagement, and shared responsibility. Philip Slater describes them in his book, *The Pursuit of Loneliness*, as the wish to live in trust and fraternal co-operation with one's fellows in a total and visible collective entity; the wish to come directly to grips with social and interpersonal problems and to confront on equal terms an environment which is not composed of ego-extensions; and the wish to share responsibility for the control of one's impulses and the direction of one's life.

The frustrations of urban man, as social analysts like the neo-Freudians Erich Fromm, Karen Horney, and Harry Stack Sullivan have pointed out, are related to basic value conflicts: conflicts between self and society, freedom and authority, competition and fraternal love; and between materialistic aspirations and choices about how to fulfil them. These value conflicts, along with their neurotic manifestations, express themselves as well in the political dilemmas of modern man. Individuals increasingly find themselves confronting an abstract entity – the 'system' or the 'establishment' – which they feel rules and frustrates their lives. They feel that the sacred symbols of the past are tarnished or worthless, and that man is split into a series of static roles, each with its own laws. They feel increasingly removed from the institutions which determine and uphold these laws, e.g. the government and the industrial organization which no longer represent human beings but things. Some escape to an inner reality through drugs and mysticism; others through cultural revolt in the form of communes, love-ins, and soul music. And a significant minority become political radicals struggling to redress the inequalities of urban industrial societies.

Poverty and Inequality

Urban society is a gigantic productive unit with a distributive system that allocates assets like income, property, education, prestige, and power. Broad inequalities exist. The lowest 20 per cent of American families receive 5 per cent of the total national income, while the highest 20 per cent receive 45 per cent. In the case of higher education, 87 per cent of the children of families with incomes of $15,000 or more attend college, compared with 41 per cent of children in middle-income homes, and 20 per cent in those earning less than $3,000 a year. In Britain, it is estimated by Professor Richard Titmuss, a well-known analyst of social welfare conditions, that a tiny minority own most of the personal wealth. The top 1 per cent of the population owns 42 per cent of all personal net capital and the top 5 per cent own the lion's share, 75 per cent. Even these proportions are underestimates of the tremendous gaps between the 'haves', the 'have-less', and the 'have-nots'. They leave out holdings and investments in pension funds and trusts, which have grown enormously in recent years, and the increasing tendency of large owners of property to distribute their wealth among their families, to spread it over time, to send it abroad, and to transform it in other ways.

Severe poverty, inadequate incomes, and insecurity are the enduring facts of life for millions of urban dwellers, despite remarkable improvements in the material welfare of many of their fellow citizens. We now know better than to naïvely assume that 'the poor' are disinherited because of family mismanagement, feckless breeding, and fathers who will not work. The majority of the urban poor are low-income, chronically unemployed workers, large and single-parent households, the aged and disabled, and disadvantaged minorities. Life is for many of them a daily struggle for survival against poverty. The poverty of unemployment, rootlessness, sickness, homelessness, and malnutrition. The poverty of culture, educational opportunity, and schools which turn out illiterate, unskilled, and deprived youth. The poverty of neighbourhood environments and housing. The poverty of pauperization in which the character withers, initiative is destroyed, and ambition is squelched.

Food and subsistence projects and welfare programmes 'to curb city poverty', far from elevating the poor into the mainstream of life, may in fact be a way of creating and maintaining a chronic state of dependency. Welfare has many purposes, as Richard Titmuss points out in his essay 'Poverty versus Inequality':

Welfare may be used to serve military and racial ends – as in Hitler's Germany. More medical care was provided by state and voluntary agencies not because of a belief in every man's uniqueness but because of a hatred of men. Welfare may be used to narrow allegiances, not to diffuse them – as in employers' fringe benefit systems. Individual gain and political quietism, fostered by the new feudalism of the corporation, may substitute for the sense of common humanity nourished by systems of non-discriminatory mutual aid.

Many well-intentioned forms of supportive welfare services cannot be adequately used by some urban dwellers simply because they cannot afford them. A widowed mother in a Boston slum clearly indicated this point when she described 'Life Like It Is in the Alley' to the psychiatrist Robert Coles:

My kids, they get sick. The welfare worker, she sends a nurse here and she tells me we should be on vitamins and the kids need all kind of check-ups. Once she took my daughter and told her she had to have her teeth looked at and the same with Peter. So, I went with my daughter and they didn't see me that day, but they said they could in a couple of weeks. And I had to pay the woman next door to mind the little ones, and there was the car fare, and we sat and sat, like before. So, I figured, it would take more than we've got to see that dentist. And when the nurse told us we'd have to come back a few times – that's how many, a few – I thought that no one ever looked at my teeth and they're not good, I'll admit, but you can't have everything, that's what I say, and that's what my kids have to know, I guess.

The plight of women, especially as urban workers, is part of the general problem of social inequality. That some women have risen to top jobs equal to men, and many more are educationally prepared for entry into male-dominated sectors of industry, politics, commerce, and the arts, is indisputably true. Yet it is also true that the large mass of urban women, whether as housewives, domestics, office and factory workers, charwomen, or the like, remain underpaid and less rewarded than men in terms of prestige, deference, respect, and esteem. Male chauvinism, increasingly exposed by radical women's liberation movements, is but one element in a general pattern of sexual, cultural, economic, and political domination which serves to suppress changes in the family structure and female self-expression and development. Media hawkers sell their products – brassières and girdles, pills and tonics – on a platform which views femininity as a chronic illness like epilepsy or diabetes. The office, once viewed by post-Victorian prudes as an escape for promiscuous libertines, is now a female ghetto where millions of clerical helots work at menial and subservient tasks: coffee-making, filing, and consoling the boss. It is probable that over the past decades women have not been closing the gap between their opportunities and rewards and those of men.

Crime in cities is an integral and exploitative part of urban culture. Organized crime takes billions from the private and public purse. Respectable businessmen and professionals reap benefits from white-collar crimes like tax evasion, falsified 'business expenses', embezzlement, and fraud. In the permissive criminal areas to which gambling, prostitution, and drugs are banished, violent crimes are on the increase. Homicide, assault, rape, and robbery are the crimes of the poorer districts, the slums and the ghettos. High arrest rates occur in the fifteen to twenty-four age group, and dramatic increases in assaults and robberies have been noted among children aged ten to fourteen years. Rising rates of social delinquency in inner-city areas, so little understood, are in large part a massive response to the urban culture of deceit, graft, and corruption. Slum dwellers exposed daily to hustlers, beats, junkies, pimps, and whores see the vaunted urban society as a big 'con game'. They 'know' that law enforcement often takes second place to corruption and that the street patrolman is often the lowest rung in a hierarchy of corruption encompassing political bosses, criminals, judges, prosecutors, and the system of patronage which holds the pyramid together.

Blocked Opportunity

The inequalities of metropolitan economic development and social change exacerbate existing tensions. Millions of beleaguered city dwellers find the escape routes from obsolescence to opportunity blocked on all fronts: bad housing, deprived environments, and distressing family conditions; discriminatory practices; defective schooling; impermanent low-paid jobs lacking apprenticeship chances and on-the-job training; opposition by established trade unions; enforced migrancy to follow job opportunities; lack of effective leadership; and exploitation by private and public employment agencies.

Racial, religious, and class conflicts intensify and break out in ugly disorders. In London's Notting Hill, the scene of racial rioting between whites and blacks in 1958, West Indian and Irish workers compete with British workers for scarce accommodation at exorbitant prices. Urban renewal districts in Liverpool and Leeds in 1972 erupted in teenage and adult violence against upwardly mobile West Indian families. As unemployment mounts and the principle of 'last in, first out' is applied against black and foreign workers by industries, local authorities, and trade unions, Britain's inner-city areas of heavy immigrant concentration face an uneasy decade ahead in human relations. At the moment, it looks as if the trend is towards greater status segregation. 'Cities are created and nourished by immigrants, yet never welcome them,' says Elizabeth Burney, a staff writer for *The Economist*, in her book *Housing on Trial*. Therefore, they set two contrasting tests for urban society:

They test the readiness to open the path of opportunity to people whose background and ways of setting about things are not those generally accepted as normal. And they test the extent to which allowances are made, and redress attempted, towards those large numbers of the urban working class whose drive has been dissipated in the sheer struggle for survival.

Major cities in the European Common Market countries face similar problems. In the poorer districts of Belgian, Dutch, German, and French cities immigrant workers from the underdeveloped belly of Europe – Southern Italy, Greece, Yugoslavia, Portugal, and Turkey – are victimized by special discriminatory statutes. In the summer of 1972, in the Afrikaander central district of Rotterdam, gangs of youths attacked shops and homes in the small Turkish community.

'The New Proles of Europe' have yet to overcome the hazards of their precarious status. Germany's immigrant foreign workers are a key factor in her rapid rise in industrial prowess. 'They help us to earn our daily bread,' said Chancellor Willi Brandt. But in legal terms they are *Gastarbeiter*, temporary guest workers, a strategic but transient element in the German policy of *Konjunkturpuffer*, by which foreign labour is imported when needed and re-exported during recession. Hence they have few rights to family housing, sickness benefits, and accident compensation. They get instead accommodation in long barrack-like quarters provided by employers like Mercedes Benz and Volkswagen, the automotive companies, or Bosch, the big electrical concern. The rules are three men to a 12'-by-6' room for 360 Deutschmarks a month with 'No whores and no politics allowed'.

In Dutch cities, Surinamese and West Indians live in overcrowded, old, high-rent areas like Pyp in Amsterdam. The most successful of them have taken up housing in Bylmereer, a new 18,000-resident government-built housing estate. The flats in the fifteen-storey towers are expensive, so many families take in lodgers. The estate has few facilities and is far from the city and jobs. Without a huge investment in building maintenance and amenities, Bylmereer, an experiment in housing and racial relations, is destined to be one of the largest slums in Europe.

The housing problems of immigrant workers in Parisian *bidonvilles* have been declared a public scandal, and when Prime Minister M. Chaban-Delmas visited one in which four Africans died in 1970, he was visibly shocked. Living conditions are barely tolerable, and few workers can hope to escape them, according to a recent exposé by Jonathan Power in the *Observer Magazine* (London). His recorded interview with one of the residents of the notorious St-Denis *bidonville*, Maria Martins Conde, the wife of a Portuguese road sweeper, brings this out clearly:

She told me that she had been living in *bidonvilles* for nine years. Now she is living in one in St-Denis. I asked her why she had left Portugal. 'There is no land,' she said, 'no opportunities.' Incredulously, I asked her if anything could be worse than this. 'Here we have money. In Portugal we had nothing.' Her two-room wood and cardboard shack was the best in the *bidonville*; she had lived there longer than most. But it had no toilet and no running water. There was one tap for the sprawling community of 2,000 people. The lavatory was a mud channel that wound itself in half-circles around the shacks. Even if it rained the sewer did not get a decent douche since all the filth agglomerated on the corners. Outside Maria's shack, a mere fifty yards away, workmen were building a new tower block. It was, apparently, mainly for French workers, although 10 per cent of the places would be kept for foreign workers.

Suddenly, and brutally, the interview came to an end, says Mr Power:

As we stood watching the foreign workers building the new flats they were most unlikely to live in, a bulldozer edged up alongside us. We were told to move. It was going to knock down some of the shacks to make way for the building operation. Quietly, without fuss, the shacks toppled over. The tenants had been warned only two days before that their homes were to be destroyed.

Studies by social scientists like Professor Arnold Rose of the University of Minnesota and Stephen Castles of the University of Essex support Jonathan Power's observations. Immigrants in urban areas live in the worst housing and pay relatively high rents. They do not get into public housing schemes for families with modest incomes like *Habitations à Loyer Moderé – H.L.M.* Others find a humble abode in special government-built hostels, many of them 'reserved' for Algerians or Africans, or *hôtels meubles* where single rooms are let to from four to eight workers or to whole families. A very large unknown number live in Parisian cellars and *bidonvilles*. One sample survey carried out by the Préfecture de Paris in 1969 discovered 37,000 persons living in *bidonvilles*, over 90 per cent of whom were 'foreigners'. Half the population were North Africans, a quarter were Portuguese, and the remainder included gypsies, Yugoslavs and other southern Europeans, and many poor Frenchmen.

The presence of immigrants in cities provokes the wrath of even the most racially tolerant Frenchmen. Definite anti-immigrant prejudices exist especially among workers and low-income groups. North Africans, particularly Algerians, generate the most hostility, according to a public opinion poll by the Institut Français d'Opinion Publique. Italians are most acceptable, with Spaniards and Portuguese in second place, and ambivalent paternalistic attitudes are held towards black Africans from Mali, Senegal, and Dahomey. Extreme hostility is shown towards immigrants who complain about their living and working conditions to their embassies and the authorities. Many find themselves deported or held in prolonged police detention. A large and undisclosed number were victimized for taking part in the General Strike of May 1968, and (according to an article in *The Review of the International Commission of Jurists*), the deportations ordered after the events took on the character of collective expulsion.

Attitudes have also hardened among members of the European Economic Community against integration of immigrant workers, despite the fact that the Articles of the Convention each has signed support the basic principle of the 'free mobility of labour' between states. The German Parliament has threatened to restrict the rights and freedoms of immigrant workers and tighten border guards and police surveillance. The Dutch are frightened of an influx of underemployed 'Black British' workers holding valid British passports, and support policies of limiting the entry of immigrants when 'certain difficulties arise in the social situation'. The Belgian Ministry of Justice can use its unlimited powers of deportation at will and the British have already established restrictive legislation in the form of the Immigration Act of 1971. Opposition to these restrictive policies has developed slowly among a small number of workers' associations, trade unions, and aid organizations like the League for the Defence of the Rights of Man. M. Marc Kock, a lawyer and secretary-general of the League, recently announced that his goal is an 'open society for foreign workers', and special attention is being given to enabling them to achieve the fullest housing, social, political, and legal rights. If they do not, then Europe's 'New Proles' will become part of a slum-shocked marginal group of 10 million in an active population of 75 million on whose back the Community will build its prosperity.

In America, no one can deny that some groups have made it up the ladder of success. Immigrant workers who at one time faced appalling urban conditions and fierce resistance, the Jews for instance, have in large part erased that episode from their collective memory. For example, who would believe today that the United Hebrew Charities Annual Report for 1901 could have said:

A condition of chronic poverty is developing in the Jewish community of New York that is appalling in its immensity. 45 per cent of our applicants, representing between 20,000 and 25,000 human beings, have been in the United States over five years, have been given the opportunities for economic and industrial improvement which this country affords; yet, notwithstanding all this, have not managed to reach a position of economic independence.

By dint of hard work many foreign immigrant groups were able to grasp the levers of political and economic power and gain both residential mobility and acceptance in the wider society. But the situation today is different; the newer migrants to the central city have not in their turn been able to break out of the proletarian despond. Indeed, some have not become proletarians at all.

In Chicago, for example, as European immigrant families adapted to the new urban culture and language and acquired an economic foothold they steadily moved into more desirable areas of second settlement farther from the centre of the city. Jews went to North Lawndale, Italians moved steadily west, the Poles and Bohemians moved southwest, the Irish and Lithuanians went south, and the Germans and Scandinavians moved northwest. Those who attained wealth left their unsuccessful kinsmen behind. Wealthy Jewish merchants and businessmen moved out north to Albany Park and Rogers Park, and better-educated German Jews settled in Hyde Park and South Shore close to the University of Chicago. Bohemian skilled workers went west to Berwyn. German machinists went to the far north-west corners of the city. Polish middle-income workers moved to nearby Cicero. Successful Irish politicians, civil servants, tavern keepers, and lawyers headed for the southern suburbs. Italian and Greek professionals – doctors, accountants, restaurant owners, and undertakers – moved to Austin, Oak Park, River Forest, Elmwood Park, and Westchester.

Meanwhile new black migrants to the city moved into the vacated central areas and struck up an uneasy relationship with the working-class Poles and Bohemians who stayed behind to defend their hard-won homes and six-storey apartment houses. Paradoxically, the Poles, who sixty years ago were the butt of racialist jokes, had the highest rates of crime and delinquency, and furnished the data for a major study of immigrant problems by William I. Thomas and Florian Znaniecki, *The Polish Peasant in America*, are now the defenders of 'The American's right to keep his neighbourhood white, free, and pure'. Today's Poles are concerned with protection of their jobs, residential values, schools, and other attributes of achieved middle-class status. They perceive a threat to this status and to the law and order which maintains it from other ethnic minorities, chiefly blacks who have recently come into the area. And they are prepared to defend their 'turf' against all comers.

Blocked opportunity in Chicago is not due to some abstract failing of those who are black and poor. It is an elemental part of a total urban system of domination. Chicago is a good ex-ample of the way in which some first-generation immigrants achieved better jobs, houses, and status. But any suggestion that this pattern holds true for the central-city slum-dwelling blacks who succeeded them has been soundly denied by most analysts of the Chicago power structure. Who gets what in Chicago today depends to a large extent on four explosive factors: nationality, race, religion, and politics.

Chicago is America's Melting Pot *par excellence*, but the ethnic groups have not melted. Each is a tight group of kinsmen prone to fear and to manipulation by community leaders against other social groups. Chicago is a segregated city divided between 2½ million whites and 1 million blacks, with a sharp line of demarcation between the affluent white suburbs and the heavily populated poor central-city black areas. Chicago is also the seat of the largest Roman Catholic archdiocese and it affects all decisions made in politics, law, education, and cultural life. Chicago is run by a strong political boss, Mayor Richard Daley, and a powerful entrenched Democratic party machine. Graft and corruption are widespread and serve to 'keep things quiet', and to maintain allegiances and a horde of incompetent touts and hangers-on. Under these conditions, the majority of slum-dwelling blacks face almost insurmountable odds in their quest for better housing, jobs, and education. They are poor, Protestant, and without power in the metropolitan religious and political structure. Meanwhile their numbers grow, fed daily by streams of new migrants to the city, and being black in Chicago means living as a dependent, exploited, despised race in an underdeveloped urban wasteland.

Black Ghetto Revolt

In American cities, the hardening race-class system, or 'colour line against black workers', has reduced large numbers of them to the status of paupers. Black anger, constantly fed by unrelieved frustrations, has given way to aggression. A major reason was the stunning failure of the civil rights movement led by Dr Martin Luther King. Another was the rise of militant Black Power ideologies. A new mood of self-esteem and racial pride developed among black youth. They fashioned a cause from the '*machismo*' culture of the ghetto – the swaggering '*Don't mess with me man*' attitude one finds among youth in deprived areas. They took up the slogans of the Black Muslim sect, the Nation of Islam, which preached 'Separatism – some of this earth or death', borrowed the 'community control' idea from the vocabulary of radical social workers and city planners, and substituted 'Black Power' and a rhythmic swinging cry of 'Black is beautiful' for the hymns and spirituals of their fathers and mothers. In the process, manifestations of black discontent changed from an isolated big-city act of rage, like the Harlem and Brooklyn, New York, riots of 1964, to widespread major incidents in scores of smaller cities.

Allegations of police brutality and unprovoked shootings are constant themes. Protests and disorders normally follow. Rioting and looting are directed against the properties of 'rent-gouging landlords', shopkeepers selling inferior goods at high prices, and discriminatory job practices.

Popular views about what causes urban racial unrest have proved under examination to be false. The often-used disclaimer by city mayors that 'small groups of outside agitators and communists have infiltrated our fair city and inoculated our good blacks with the virus of racism' does not seem to hold water. *Who Riots?*, a study by Massachusetts Institute of Technology and Columbia University social scientists, showed that in each case local grievances had been mounting for years and were considered real issues of blatantly ignored civil rights. Local activists served as riot leaders, and their actions were justified by large sections of the community as a necessary act of defiance against remote authority.

Another study, *Racial Attitudes in Fifteen American Cities*, carried out by the Institute for Social Research of the University of Michigan, indicated a decided contrast in black and white attitudes on crucial issues like racial integration versus Black Power. Half the blacks interviewed supported the moderate programme of their traditional spokesman, the National Association for the Advancement of Coloured People. This was unexpectedly low. A surprising one third of those interviewed backed the militant 'Freedom now' and Black Power separatist views of young radicals like Stokely Carmichael. Whites, on the other hand, overwhelmingly supported gradual legislative reforms in housing and racial discrimination. The increasing polarization of urban blacks and whites was sharply illustrated again on the local level by a study completed by Professor Peter Rossi of Johns Hopkins University. Probing into strife-torn ghettos in major cities, Rossi interviewed the 'servants of the community': policemen, teachers, shopkeepers, welfare workers, political party workers, and employers. He uncovered a deep current of cynicism and insensitivity to the needs of local people. And he concluded that 'if these are the faces that American institutions present to the ghetto, then the alienation of the ghetto from the main community is scarcely to be wondered at'.

The new predominance of black populations in the central areas of American cities offers them a chance for political control over the economic and social resources necessary for the elevation of the people. Since the population of some eleven main cities will become nearly 50 per cent black in the next fifteen years, the omens for black control are promising. Euphoric reactions to these trends have come from many quarters. Stokely Carmichael said at a mass rally during an election in East St Louis, 'Let me tell you, baby, when we get 52 per cent of the voters in a city, we own that city – lock, stock, and barrel.' Political parties have offered more token participation, and some municipalities have elected black mayors or a few black members to local councils. Big business and universities, urged on by government, speak of committing their technological leadership to conquering 'the racial problem'. The leaders of Xerox, General Motors, Polaroid, and Chrysler are portrayed as being involved in bettering race relations, creating manpower-training programmes, and boosting black capitalism in the ghettos. Skilled analysts of urban economics and politics, brought into the fray, see optimistic possibilities for blacks. For example, they point out that Chicago, Hartford, New York, and other big cities are investing billions of dollars into rebuilding downtown areas. In Detroit, Henry Ford has announced a massive $·2 billion plan to revitalize the centre. In Gary, Indiana, the great Midwestern steel town that elected a black mayor, Richard Hatcher, U.S. Steel has announced it has no plans to move. Thus in another decade, if not before, some observers say this investment can be used by black politicians as a lever for political purposes. City finances might also get a recharge if federal revenues are made available for municipal use.

The pessimists say that this will have little effect on other trends, i.e. the white middle-class exodus to the suburbs, the decline of urban tax bases, and the flight of key industries from the city. Furthermore, the vaunted business contribution may be nothing more than a sham. Most manpower programmes are little more than experimental and demonstration projects involving a handful of disadvantaged and hard-core unemployed individuals. Industrialists and their managers are parts of multinational corporations operating in the world market. They are skilled in systems analysis and act upon market trends discerned through computerized surveys. They do not depend on the mandate of any commonweal. Therefore profitless social engineering remains for most corporations little more than a public relations sideline.

If this ideal of black central-city control fails, black militants are now aware that American cities are vulnerable. And there is much talk of a ghetto revolt. After all, it is said, Bedford–Stuyvesant, Harlem, and Newark are a black crescent around Manhattan's centre and straddle key transportation and daily commuter routes. In Chicago's South Side every fourth street is commercial. Arsonists could set off fires in the principal white-owned businesses, thereby occupying the fire and police departments while well-trained saboteurs spread out over the city to blow up power plants, despoil water systems, and derail trains – most of which run through the ghetto. In Detroit, the East Side has several vital installations, including electricity and water plants and the Chrysler car-making and Parke-Davis pharmaceutical industries. Philadelphia's ghetto areas command the communication route from Washington to New York, border vital industrial areas, and surround the University of Pennsylvania and Drexel Tech complex, including a major railway and post office centre.

When Rap Brown, a black militant, said to an incredulous audience some years ago, 'Violence is as American as apple pie', he was referring not only to the mounting pattern of armed aggression in cities, but also to the general climate of violence that permeates each stage of American history: revolutionary violence, Civil War violence, the Indian Wars, vigilante violence, agrarian and labour violence, and military and police violence. Now America seems hell-bent on bringing a new stage of its history into birth, or preventing its entry – through the barrel of a gun. The deepening problem of armed violence between differing groups of citizens will therefore affect the future prospects of American cities. At the moment it looks to some political observers that cities will be composed of fortified enclaves. Central business districts, surrounded by decaying and increasingly black neighbourhoods, will be constantly under siege for fear of terrorists and marauding gangs of youths. Streets and residential neighbourhoods will be unsafe. Ghetto slum areas will be 'free territories' perhaps out of police control during night-time hours. Armed guards will protect all public facilities such as schools, libraries, and playgrounds, and deputized security police will 'ride shotgun' on all public transport. High-rise, high-income apartment buildings and residential compounds will be protected by private armies, savage guard dogs, and electronic devices. The ownership of guns will be universal in the white suburbs; home defences will include window grilles, audio-visual scanning devices, and infra-red cameras to spot night-time intruders; armed citizens in cars will supplement inadequate police patrols. High-speed patrolled expressways will be sanitized corridors connecting safe areas, and private automobiles, taxicabs, and commercial vehicles will be routinely equipped with unbreakable glass, light armour, and other security features.

Violence-prone Cities

In affluent urban society, with all its resources and high levels of consumption and standards of living, widespread poverty and inequality and a plethora of anxiety-based disorders indicate that something is deeply wrong. Within the last two decades vociferous opposition has grown against modern urban civilization. A mood of rebellion developed among young students, unemployed youth, and war veterans. For them the crisis of personal and social estrangement in cities is only the representation on the metropolitan scale of deeper societal problems. And they call for nothing less than a radical restructuring of all productive and marketing relations, government and education, and of the basic beliefs and values of man in an age of predatory technology.

Militant students draw police and troops into open confrontation on the streets. Cars, trams, and buses are turned over and burned to block streets and disrupt traffic. Attack squads occupy or raid the headquarters of communications industries, newspapers, banks, and large multinational corporations. Centrally located universities and schools provide thousands of potential recruits for marching and fighting. Terrorist groups hurl their grievances into the political arena in a hail of fire-bombs. They proclaim their view that 'there is only one way to a life of love and freedom: to attack and destroy the racist, sexist, imperialist forces of death and exploitation and to build a just society – REVOLUTION'. As a result the citadels of power are under siege, and the culture and politics of cities are vigorously contested.

The halcyon years of student protest in the world's major cities, notably Paris, Mexico City, and Tokyo, were 1968–70. *Les événements* of May and June 1968 in Paris were probably the closest thing to insurrectionary outbreak in recent times in a

Western city. Student–youth demonstrations at universities and schools and on the streets coincided with industrial work stoppages that virtually developed into a general strike. Paris and France itself were brought to a standstill. President de Gaulle left Paris to confer with his generals in the French Army H.Q. as a quarter of a million Parisians paraded through the streets in a massive demonstration of their discontent. Meanwhile M. Pompidou negotiated the vital wage increases with Communist trade union leaders which saved the country from chaos and put 9 million strikers back on the job. So, the revolution was co-opted by the political leadership of the leftist parties, which chose to keep political decision-making within the confines of the party and off the streets. French factory workers were not prepared to go as far as the students; their own demands were oriented primarily towards fuller participation in French society rather than the overthrow of it. The hoped-for student–worker front was disrupted when workers accepted concessions to their immediate demands and the students were unable to propose positive alternative demands that might have held their allies, or attracted new ones, for further struggle.

Mexico City had its worst disorders for fifty years during a four-month strike by 150,000 university and high school students in the summer and autumn of 1968. Students fought running battles with riot police and troops supported by tanks and armoured cars. By the end of July the students succeeded in closing every secondary, undergraduate, and postgraduate school and were in occupation of the National University and the Polytechnic Institute. Walls and bulletin boards were plastered with revolutionary mottoes and quotations of Mao Tse-tung. Students renamed the auditorium of the School of Philosophy and Letters in honour of the slain Cuban revolutionary hero, Ernesto Che Guevara, and classroom doors were painted with the names of Ho Chi Minh, Fanon, and Lenin. In October fierce battles took place as government forces drew students out on to the streets. A decisive struggle erupted in the central Plaza of the Three Cultures located in the Nonoalco-Tlatelolco housing project. Finally, after much bloodshed, government forces smashed student resistance and the disorder was put down as the Olympic Games began.

Left-wing Tokyo students took over major universities and higher education centres for varying periods during 1969. Classes were halted and pitched battles took place with the police. Students were led by the Maoist section of the *Zengakuren*, the All-Japan Federation of Students' Councils, with support from an alliance of young Trotskyists, anarchists, and socialists. Student militants viewed the flaws in the educational system as symptomatic of the 'profit-first disease that runs like a cancer through Japanese society'. Their grievances were directed at first at bad housing conditions and alleged corruption in the system of entrance fees. They demanded a voice in school affairs. Later, as the struggle broadened to encompass an attack on the whole structure of society, the students claimed that 'reform is not possible within the present framework; the framework itself must be destroyed'.

Major world cities are prone to terrorist violence too. They are part of urbanized societies whose most affluent conservative sections are unresponsive to growing pockets of economic distress and social injustice, resist change, and sow the conditions for armed resistance and revolution. West Berlin has been a theatre of political violence and bomb attacks for years. Milan is still recuperating from a wave of sabotage which culminated in the mysterious death of the left-wing publisher Feltrinelli. Britain has her troubles in Belfast, Northern Ireland, where both the I.R.A. and Provisionals, and the Protestant Ulster Defence Association have raised urban guerrilla warfare to the level of a grim and fatal art.

Political violence has increased in Latin American cities. The Tupamaros of Montevideo have dramatically developed urban guerrilla techniques. In Rio de Janeiro, the National Liberation Alliance demonstrates that urban guerrilla resistance can challenge the toughest military regime. Guerrilla groups like the Monteneros in Buenos Aires and Rosario raid, rob, bomb, kidnap, and occasionally kill. They are young and middle class; their ideology, a curious mixture of Peronism, Communism, and anti-Americanism. Their immediate targets are the 'repressive forces of the state', particularly the police. And the police reply to terror with terror. They too kidnap and kill and maim and torture.

In North America, Canadian cities have been focal points of political violence. Montreal, for example, is the centre of activities of separatist groups and left-wing movements like the *Front de Libération du Québec – F.L.Q*. Their supporters come from the ranks of Maoist and Trotskyist students. Bombing attacks have been mainly directed at institutions like the Montreal Stock Exchange and the Canadian defence headquarters in Ottawa. The *F.L.Q.* claim to represent the frustration and discontent of French Canadians who were looked upon by their Anglo-Saxon economic masters as inferior people. They seek the establishment of a free socialist French existence in Canada and the equality of the two languages and cultures.

A rise in terrorist activities has also taken place in violence-prone American cities. There is little doubt that some of it is caused by right-wing anti-Communist groups with leanings towards the Ku Klux Klan, the Minutemen, and the John Birch Society. In addition, black nationalist groups like the Revolutionary Action Movement in New York and the Weathermen, a splinter group from the white radical Students for a Democratic Society, are held responsible for scores of bomb explosions. Their targets were the headquarters of international companies lodged in midtown New York skyscrapers, like Mobil Oil, International Business Machines, and Chase Manhattan Bank. Other targets were symbols of the 'establishment' – government offices, police stations, Reserve Officer Training Corps centres at universities, and various military installations in major cities all over the country.

Violence in the city has led to heavy emphasis on repressive police measures. Most big-city forces have a reserve contingent of riot police, similar to the French *Garde Mobile*. Some are creating special city armies with tanks and heavy weapons. Law enforcement is a hard-sell industry with a wide range of 'convincers' and 'persuaders'. There are high-velocity rubber bullets, CS gas pocket grenades, and lead-filled sap gloves for the policeman who likes to club, gun, or gas his man as efficiently as possible. In addition, there is a glittering range of armour-plated vehicles to tempt forces to keep one step ahead of each other. The MPPV, for example, is the Rolls-Royce of the law-enforcement business – a mobile barracks that you do not have to steer around anything you'd rather squash.

This violence on the urban scale reflects in many ways violence on the national and international scale. When urban industrial society is exploding in violence on its campuses, in its factories, its ghettos, and in far-off corners of the world, there is no other possibility for its cities than violence. A society that has produced all kinds of segregation – racial, class, generational, economic, and intellectual – has to produce a violent and degraded human environment. The city has, as a consequence, to become a very dangerous place to live in.

Dialectics of Disorder

Taking one's grievances into the streets is a historical mode of political action. Before the establishment of parliamentary democracy in Europe the streets were the legitimate arena for the expression of popular demands by the unorganized masses. In time more sophisticated forms of political action through trade unions and working-class parties took their place. Today's street riots, demonstrations, and violence expose real institutional failures in modern urban society and may become the forerunner of a new stage of democratic reform – by armed insurrection and rebellion.

At the moment a conflict rages among architects and planners who are in search of an organizing principle for relating urban planning policies to the unmet needs and aspirations of urban man. Two recent books mirror this conflict. One, entitled *With Man in Mind*, is by Constance Perin, a former editor of the *Journal of the American Institute of Planners* and Fulbright Fellow at the Bartlett School, University College, London. The other is *The Uses of Disorder* by Dr Richard Sennett, a Harvard-educated urban sociologist. Miss Perin seeks to redesign cities in collaboration with social scientists to meet human needs. She asks, 'What do we need to know in order to design with man in mind?' and 'How can we learn to specify the human properties any new physical environment is to respond to?' In proposing the answers Miss Perin covers a wide range of American and British literature in architecture, planning, and sociology. The reader is treated to insights gained from compiled lists of 'basic needs', 'essential striving sentiments', 'amenity attributes', and 'site planning elements'. Typical daily activities, like the shopping behaviour of housewives in high-rise dwellings, are scanned sequentially with the sharp detail of a time-lapse camera. Her book portrays, however, a conflictless view of urban social change, and many of the authors cited speak of the 'resolution of urban social problems' with the forked tongue of ad-glib America. They abhor, but avoid coming to grips with the basic nitty-gritty: endemic poverty, race-class segregation, blocked opportunity, naked aggression, the evils of political and economic systems, and the adolescent self-slavery which makes up so much of urban life.

Whereas Miss Perin seeks the regularization, albeit humanistically, of urban man's behaviour, Dr Sennett wants more diversity and change, not stability. He says that the growth of affluent communities creates among middle-income, middle-aged parents and many of their children an acceptance of safe and secure self-slavery within repressive systems of law and order. Much of urban planning and design merely recapitulates this fact and endorses the exploitative relations between the suburban dwelling victimizer and the slum-locked victim. He proposes (with distant echoes of the 'permanent revolution' of Mao Tse-tung and Che Guevara) the creative use of all forms of disorder as the only dynamic mechanism left for ushering in a non-repressive, libertarian urban society.

Sennett is clearly influenced by the 'self-through-struggle' concepts of Erik Erikson. Using Erikson's concept of the identity crisis – the conscious attempt to reconcile self and modern society – he presents a psychoanalytically oriented defence of dissent and revolt, particularly by militant students, blacks, and poor whites. Furthermore, he claims that the revolutionary passage must be an emotional experience through conflict/disorder/suffering/pain/challenge/response/transcendence – that not only rids society of repression but radically transforms bureaucratic structures.

When more conflict takes place in the public sphere, when the technocratic and bureaucratic routines are socialized in the image of emerging forces, says Dr Sennett, the product of disorder will be a greater sensitivity to the problems of connecting public service to urban needs. He concludes that 'the fruit of this conflict – a paradox which is the essence of this book – is that in extricating the city from pre-planned control, men will become more in control of themselves and more aware of each other. That is the promise and the justification of disorder.'

Our discussion so far has indicated the widespread character of urban conflict and violence. What emerges is that there are many interacting causes perceived by many different observers. Historians and political scientists speak of class conflict, inefficient government, and unresponsive political elites.

Sociologists are exploring the urban 'reservoirs of frustration', and patterns of relative deprivation as measured by differences on the 'want–get ratio'. Social psychologists are examining the way that frustration turns into anger and aggression.

What seems most apparent and plausible is that social conflict and violence are products of the political system. It arises from a rational evaluation by aggrieved urban dwellers of the continued failure of political systems to deliver the goods and benefits in a manner seen as responsive and responsible. This gap, and it is a big one, between the theory and practice of government is, ultimately, the basic cause of urban violence.

6   Search for Solutions

In all the major cities of the world the same large question marks hang over the heads of politicians, administrators, and urban planners. How to plan and regulate the competition for land and living space? How to deal with volatile discontent in the heart of the city, sclerosis in its major arteries, and the rag-bag of scattered development on its outer fringes? A variety of weapons are or will be at hand to tackle problems of movement and congestion, decay and sprawl, and metropolitan regional development. New laws, land use regulation, increased welfare services, and computerized 'think-tanks' are all applied to urban design and policy-making.

But political inertia, vested interests, and increasing financial costs are powerful inhibiting factors. Municipalities, industrial giants, and public utility companies resist reform. Ill-informed publics are easily stampeded into voting for candidates who do not represent their needs. There is an all-too-common, cavalier and *ad hoc* approach to urban problems. Moreover, the heavy emphasis on technological and manipulative solutions indicates a frightening inability among professionals and politicians to deal with critical issues, or even to fully comprehend what they are doing. Under these conditions, it is hopeless to propose solutions to the crisis of cities without instituting fundamental changes in the structure of public decision-making, especially metropolitan government, planning, and citizen participation.

New Movement in the City

In the future cities will have to cope with immense problems of congestion on already crowded corridors of movement. One of the goals of transport engineers and planners will be to make possible the speedy, safe, and comfortable movement of more people in, out of, and around cities, and to reduce the volume of cars and noxious vehicles on the streets.

In the field of mass transit the introduction of electronically automated trains, signalling controls, and fare collection methods will improve journey times and operating costs. Mass transit systems incorporating these innovations are being planned in Santiago and Calcutta, where newly designed trains will carry payloads of 30,000 passengers per hour at speeds up to 80 m.p.h. There is also a new wave of interest in designing efficient tramways like the Tram-Métro, U-bahn, and Stadtbahn systems in European cities. With maximum carrying capacities of 25,000 passengers travelling at speeds of 40–50 m.p.h., improved and modernized tramways may find a new place in city transport planning.

Administrators and planners, searching for new ways of moving people within cities, have created ingenious electronic and engineering solutions to rearrange and improve passenger journeys. On the horizon are a host of smaller, fully automated transport forms tailor-made to fit the personal needs of users. Passengers will be able to travel almost directly to their destinations in small carriages operated by electronic guidance equipment on overhead or surface mono-rails. One example, is the 'guided busway', a series of small buses which seat four to twenty people and are guided along fixed railways at 12 m.p.h. During peak hours, the buses make scheduled stops, but in off-peak hours they can be used like an automatic elevator. The passenger 'calls' the vehicle by pressing a button in the station and after boarding the bus presses another button to indicate his destination. Another example is the 'auto-taxi service' using four-seater, electric-powered cars travelling on tracks in a transparent tube. Running directly to and from a central marketing depot at average speeds of 35 m.p.h., the auto-taxi could accommodate a housewife, her children, and large quantities of shopping. With its seats removed, it becomes a delivery vehicle for household goods, e.g. newspapers, mail, milk, and groceries. Tickets with destination codes on them are interpreted by a computer to route the vehicle, and stations are situated off the main track so that other auto taxis not programmed to stop can go straight through.

Personal Rapid Transport or PRT, as this novel mode has been called, is one of the newest innovations in the transport future of metropolitan areas. PRT systems can carry up to 10,000 persons per hour and can travel at an average of 35 m.p.h. They have several acknowledged advantages, according to the designers. They provide fast, frequent service between closely spaced stations, can handle large rush-hour crowds, and also provide late-night service. Already four prototype PRT systems have been exhibited in Turin, Seattle, Tokyo, and Pittsburgh and at the Washington, D.C., Transpo Exhibition in 1972; in addition, the Dallas–Fort Worth Regional Airport, one of the fastest-growing airports in America, is planning to install a PRT service for its airline passengers. Pioneers in PRT research are the aero-space companies, like Boeing and Vought Aeronautics, who desperately need new markets for their specialized skills. Westinghouse Electric, who created the Skybus guided system for Pittsburgh, is also interested. Ford Motor Company engineers are looking for new outlets for their traditional rubber-tyred technology as well as for information of use in creating a guided motorcar system. German and French firms are building PRT prototypes with governmental aid, and Britain's Hawker-Siddeley company is promoting two systems: the four-passenger Cabtrack and the twenty-passenger Mini-tran. Before these PRT systems come into widespread use, however, some basic problems will have to be solved. High capital costs are the main problem. Automation and elevated structures are expensive. And when fully operational the PRT's are expected to cost in the region of £4–£8 million per mile – hardly a competitive price advantage over the costs of full-sized mass rapid transit. Further-more, the use of many small vehicles will increase both maintenance and capital costs. It is probable that some of these costs may be offset by the fact that most PRT prototypes are rubber-tyred and run on electricity and hence are relatively silent and non-polluting. But before they are finally built, they will have to prove that they are much less objectionable and less costly than present alternatives, such as road building, restricted bus lanes, high speed trams, and improved underground transit.

Pressures are mounting to close city centres to cars and to open up new attractive spaces for pedestrians, shoppers, and leisure-time activities. Midtown Manhattan planners, for example, have proposed a string of covered public spaces along wide avenues above existing sidewalks. These *gallerie*, reminiscent of the arcades of Bologna, will connect buildings and provide traffic-free, all-season, twenty-four-hour public places filled with shops, restaurants, and theatres displaced by the current surge of office development. Campaigns to 'revitalize the centre' and to 'give downtown back to the people' emphasize the use of mechanical pedestrian conveyors, like moving pavements and travelators, to move pedestrians quickly and efficiently in high-density, no-car locations. The moving pavement will ease long journeys over horizontal distances and between floor levels. It can carry 30,000 persons per hour at 2 m.p.h. speeds, and has been used successfully on an experimental basis at heavily used air and sea terminals and at congested interchange points between rail and subway systems. Pedestrian conveyors have the advantage of being able to handle high-volume pedestrian flows and every type of passenger, including the old and infirm, the disabled, and mothers with children. For these reasons, they may have an important role to play if installed in shopping centres, car parks, supermarkets, and department stores.

Engineers and planners also have high expectations for another new mode of pedestrian movement via 'never-stop' belt systems which can carry up to 6,000 persons per hour. The Carveyor, for example, is based on a train of six-passenger cars travelling between stations at 15 m.p.h. It slows down at each station and passengers get off on to a platform moving at 1·5 m.p.h. which takes them to the exits. The Telecanape, another 'never-stop' system, uses a different approach at stations. In this case the station consists of a large circular platform which rotates so that the outer edge moves at the same speed as a train passing through the station. Passengers enter the platform from a stairway in the centre where the speed of rotation is low and then walk radially towards the outer edge and the train. The trains are a line of twelve-seater, rubber-tyred vehicles which travel on steel rails at 4 m.p.h. while encircling the revolving platform and at 8 m.p.h. between stations.

These novel modes of transport may make a valuable contribution to the revitalization of city centres and the amelioration of congestion. Coupled with traffic-management schemes, pedestrianization projects, and co-ordinated road, highway, and land-use planning, they could result in the final eviction of the noxious car from the heart of cities. Ultimately, however, the utility of improved mass transit, new personal transit, and mechanical

144

pedestrian conveyors will depend on how they help people overcome socio-economic barriers to mobility, and how they contribute to the resolution of conflicts between our daily activities and
the structures, layout, and fabric of cities.

New Towns, New Frontiers?

Governments faced with the perils of decay and sprawl are seeking ways of channelling metropolitan development into new
communities and towns. New towns are, of course, not all that
uncommon in man's history. Rulers, colonizers, and speculators have always used new settlements to serve their purposes. The ancient Greeks and Romans, the Incas and the
Yoruba, and the medieval kings of Europe used settler colonies
to expand trade and populate distant frontiers. Even in our time,
establishing new centres of economic activity in remote underdeveloped regions is an essential part of the strategy of development of many nations. In the Soviet Union, for example, more
than 800 new towns have been built for this purpose, mainly in
Siberia and Central Asia. What is unique today is the siting of
new towns around big cities as a national policy of metropolitan
planning and regional development. The British were first in the
field and now there are eight new towns surrounding London,
and others serving Glasgow, Edinburgh, Birmingham, and
Liverpool. The French are building five new towns around
Paris at Cergy-Pontoise, Evry, Trappes, Vallée de la Marne, and
Melun-Sénart. And the new town concept has now spread
widely and produced some innovative settlements near big cities
in all parts of the world: Bramlea (Toronto), Tema (Accra),
Petaling Jaya (Kuala Lumpur), Farsta and Vallingby (Stockholm), and Hino (Tokyo).

However, the case of Britain, and London in particular,
deserves a more elaborate comment in this context, because its
new towns have attracted world-wide attention. Britain has a
long history of concern with problems of cities. The new town,
a postwar innovation, grows out of attempts to combine the
advantages of town and country life in both new settlements and
older communities as antidotes to the squalor and spread of
industrial towns. Enterprising nineteenth-century philanthro-
pists built workers' settlements around new factories at Saltaire

in 1853, Bournville in 1878, and Port Sunlight in 1887. Later, Letchworth (1903) and Welwyn Garden City (1920) followed from the planning concepts of Ebenezer Howard. Howard's ideas that cities should be encircled by green belts – rings of inviolate open space – to provide recreation and prevent cities merging into agglomerations, were incorporated into British town-planning law and practice. The result was the New Towns Act of 1946. Since then some thirty new towns have been built or started, and more than a million people have taken up residence in them.

The new towns have merit as living and working places in their own right, but in addition they help to limit the growth of existing nearby urban areas. They can serve to siphon off populations, 'demagnetize' the city's attraction to migrants, and deflect them to new planned locations. Sir Patrick Abercrombie, the 'father of new towns', had this very much in mind when he proposed in 1944 that London should maintain high densities of 200 per residential acre in the centre, decreasing to 136 in the inner zones and 100 on the outskirts. Since many of the inner areas had higher densities than those proposed, there remained a huge excess population of one million persons, mainly lower-income workers, who would have to be accommodated elsewhere. This was to be accomplished in new and fully planned communities, some twenty to thirty miles from the city, outside the suburbs and green belt. The same principles were applied in other large urban areas, and from this plan the new towns emerged.

The new town approach is to provide work opportunities, particularly in light industry, as well as homes. This is to prevent them from becoming dormitory suburbs of the cities whose problems they are supposed to solve. Ease of access to all community facilities is another established criterion. Typically, housing units, primary schools, clinics and welfare centres, shops, a community centre, public house, and church are available within short walking distance. Many new towns have traffic-free residential and shopping areas, and industry is sited for easy access to transport and homes.

These ideas have been extended to the planned expansion of existing towns. For example, Northampton and Ipswich, with present populations of 120,000 each, will provide accommodation for an additional 70,000 Londoners by 1981. The merit of building in existing towns lies in the savings gained from already established central-area facilities. This leaves local councils free to undertake the renewal of obsolescent areas and to replace substandard housing.

New towns have contributed some positive benefits, and are an exciting innovation. But there are continuing overspill problems in large cities which must be met. In England and Wales, there are still at least 1·8 million slum dwellings and most of them are in old congested inner-urban areas. By 1981, in London alone, about a million people will need to be housed. Rehabilitation of old areas provides the short-term answer. But because rehousing families at modern standards requires more space than is available for building within cities, most of the population will have to be relocated outside. Ultimately more accommodation in new and expanded towns will have to be built.

British planners have high hopes that the next wave of new town building will relieve the problems of older cities, and provide new living styles as well. Milton Keynes, now taking shape on 21,880 acres in north Buckinghamshire, is scheduled for completion in 1990, and will be Britain's and Europe's biggest new city. It is located between London and Birmingham and will handle the overspill populations of both cities. Total capital costs are estimated at £700 million and will be financed by the controlling government-created Milton Keynes Development Corporation (£333 million loan from the Treasury), local authorities (£169 million), and the private sector (£198 million). The plans for Milton Keynes call for a 250,000 resident population living in low-density neighbourhoods small enough for people not to feel dominated by buildings, crowds, or systems. Homes will be built eight or ten to the acre; and in line with government policy, half the homes will be for rent and half for sale at prices ranging from £5,000 to £20,000 each. Flexibility is the key philosophy of the designers. Flexibility of choice of movement via footpaths, private cars, public buses, Dial-a-Bus systems, and mono-rail within a grid framework of sixty-eight 1-km squares bounded by 'parkway-style' roads. In the city centre, 'roads will serve people, not be their masters', say Milton Keynes publicists. People will walk at ground level, and cars will be banished above or below ground where necessary – the proper place for servants' quarters. Flexibility of choice of leisure pursuits, recreation activities, and comprehensive community services will also be available. There is a linear park along waterways like the Grand Union Canal running through the city, and man-made lakes with opportunities for a range of water sports. Britain's latest innovation in mass education by audio-visual media, the Open University, is also located in Milton Keynes and will emphasize the city's contribution to the knowledge industry. To be a success, however, Milton Keynes must provide employment for its inhabitants. Failure to do so will turn the new city into a dormitory area between London and Birmingham. The hope is that 130,000 jobs will be created for semi-skilled and skilled male and female workers. If things go well they will be working in the offices, factories, and distributing houses of many relocated British firms and a number of subsidiaries of foreign firms like Hoechst, the German chemical concern, Olivetti, Kodak, and the American Can Company.

New-town enthusiasts are busily engaged in proclaiming the merits of the British experience to thousands of visitors and tourists from all over the world. But they have tended to overlook criticisms that the costs of building, operating, and maintaining new towns may be quite excessive in the light of alternative solutions to problems of urban growth and industrial development. There is also concern about the 'one-class', middle-income aspect of new towns. They are populated mainly by semi-skilled and skilled workers, clerical staff and professional and managerial personnel employed in light manufacturing, research, and science-based industries. The towns continue to attract a restricted range of technical manpower and automated industry from all over the country and Europe. Clearly, some variety in people and jobs is called for to open up opportunities in the new towns for low-income inner-city manual and low-skilled workers, particularly coloured immigrants, and to correct what may become a bad imbalance in the distribution of national productivity and employments. There is a need for continuing social research, particularly for accurate forward planning to anticipate and minimize problems created by distorted age, class, and racial structures, and the lack of fit between housing, employment, and social services. Two other points are of vital importance within the context of our discussion. Too many British new towns have failed to overcome the depressing aspects of large-scale government-sponsored settlements. Town centres lacking in character and excitement, dim barren subways under roads, the sameness and uniformity of streets and housing, the large unused communal spaces and townscapes which dribble away into uninteresting horizons – all give the impression of a vast sub-topian sprawl. Finally, though a start has been made through government initiative, the citizens of new towns cannot live forever under the patronage of the state. Soon dates must be set for the devolution of powers to the citizens of new towns and to their properly constituted local authorities.

In the United States, government support for a new towns policy has enabled the mushroom growth of more than sixty developments all over the country. Legislation passed between 1966 and 1970 provided the needed stimulus, particularly Title IV of the 1968 New Communities Act. Unlike in Britain, American new towns tend to be privately built middle and upper class communities in relatively rural places or unrelated to the problems of metropolitan blight. Large land-holding families initiated new communities at Irvine, south of Los Angeles, and at Valencia, north of the San Fernando Valley. Big business companies like Exxon Corp., Westinghouse Electric, Kaiser Aluminum, and Goodyear Tire & Rubber Company are now well established in the field. Gulf Oil Corporation has a $15 million stake in Reston, Virginia, eighteen miles west of Washington, D.C.; and U.S. Gypsum has a substantial share in Park Forest South, some thirty miles south of Chicago. The unique exceptions are Levittown, near Willingboro, New Jersey, and Columbia, Maryland, midway between Baltimore and Washington, D.C. Both were created by individual entrepreneurs. Levitt & Sons are, of course, pioneers in the privately built housing market and have long experience in the business of purchasing and consolidating parcels of land, building homes and facilities, and selling the merits of new community living. Columbia was created by James W. Rouse, a mortgage banker turned city builder, on 15,000 acres of farmland purchased from 169 separate titleholders. It is a self-sustaining 'Garden City dream community' of medium-priced, mixed-racial residences financed with $100 million that Rouse obtained from life insurance companies to back his ideas.

America's unique contribution to the new towns concept lies, however, in the current trend of combined private and public initiative in the planning of 'new towns in-town'. Scores of developers are queuing up for grants and credits of up to $50 million made available under Title VII of the 1970 Housing and

Development Act to resuscitate decaying inner-city areas and stem the emigration of middle-class families.

Battery Park City, to be located along a one-mile stretch of decaying south Manhattan waterfront, is one example of urban 'new towns in-town'. The $1 billion project is literally a city within a city – a totally self-contained community offering apartments, offices, schools, shops, parks, and even its own internal transportation system. By 1983 some 55,000 persons with mixed incomes will reside there – a population greater than twenty-three of New York State's counties. In addition two new communities with 5,000 units of mixed-income housing are scheduled to be built on Welfare Island, a weedy two-mile-long island in New York's East River. It is the brain child of the state's Urban Development Corporation and will offer some new features: a twenty-five-acre ecological study preserve, a four-mile canti-levered promenade encircling the island, and a ban on auto-mobiles. Residents will commute to the mainland via public transit and travel about the island by foot and mini buses.

Just twelve blocks from downtown Minneapolis, local developers are planning a 300-acre new community, Cedar-Riverside, for 30,000 residents. Within twenty years the new occupants will be living in low- and moderate-income apartments and elegant town houses – all connected by pedestrian skyways and leafy plazas. In Philadelphia, five firms intend to construct a fifty-acre, $400 million new town in the shadow of City Hall. Franklin Town, as it is to be called, features clusters of mixed-income residences, a spacious 'town square', and a tree-lined central boulevard bordered by shops, theatres, and restaurants. The development is expected to enrich the city with annual real estate taxes of $10 million – or twenty-eight times the current return from the area. If the new town in-town concept gains headway, say government and congressional supporters, 'it could account for half the nation's metropolitan development within ten years'.

But no one is really sure whether new towns will help resolve current urban problems, and whether they can contribute to a national urban planning policy. The National Committee on Urban Growth Policy sees new communities as essential elements of a strategy to shape urban growth. It has proposed the creation of more than 100 of them, with populations ranging from 100,000 to one million, by AD 2000. This view is supported by Professor Charles Haar of the Massachusetts Institute of Technology–Harvard University Joint Center for Urban Studies as a way of designing new patterns of living and increasing the nation's supply of housing. He also feels that new communities can meet the needs of a wide range of income groups at economical prices, and help relieve pressures on older cities. On the other hand, Jane Jacobs, a well-known writer on urban affairs, was recorded in *The New York Times Magazine* as saying 'New towns are a cop-out', and far removed from 'really getting down to the business of understanding the stagnating, possibly dying, economy of the old city and doing something about it'. New towns presently proposed in America will not solve central-area decay or suburban sprawl, and they will continue to house mainly white middle-class families and divert state and federal financial resources from the central cities. Whether new towns will ever play a different role in America will depend on how long it takes to change public opinion, particularly among middle-class voters, and to mobilize effective legislation and financial resources.

Towards Metropolitan–Regional Management

Problems of urban growth, sprawl, and congestion all have direct interlinkages with the surrounding regions of the city. More and more planners are seeking to establish broad frameworks of metropolitan–regional planning within which the local plans for cities, suburbs, new towns, and rural areas can be developed. Reports from many world cities, however, indicate that on the whole the supporting political and administrative structures for large-scale strategies tend to be weak, obsolete, or non-existent. As a result metropolitan–regional planning programmes, where they exist, usually achieve relatively modest gains, if any at all.

Tokyo's efforts are frustrated by lack of any effective methods or machinery for controlling urban and regional growth, and by immense pressure on land due to a high annual population growth and economic development. The green belt has dwindled; offices and expressways bring a torrent of motorcars into the city centre. Tokyo has a Capital Region Development Commission responsible for an area radiating from 75 to 100 kilometres from

Tokyo Station. At the head of the commission is a Minister of Construction and four members nominated by him; but they have no resources, and no effective relations or links with local or city government authorities.

Paris has tried to gain a broad perspective on urban and regional problems with the aid of two planning instruments. One is the master plan, P.A.D.O.G. – *Plan d'Aménagement et d'Organisation Générale de la Région Parisienne*; the other is a general survey of regional needs, the *Avant-Projet de Programme Duodécennal pour la Région de Paris*. Political control is in other hands, however. Ultimate responsibility for the planning of the District's affairs is held by a Prefect, called a Delegate-General, directly responsible to the Prime Minister. His administrative board composed of councillors from local communes is in practice a centrally controlled bureaucracy superimposed on an obsolete communal structure.

In Britain, the Greater London Council has come under serious criticism from central government on a number of strategic metropolitan–regional issues. The G.L.C.'s Greater London Development Plan of 1969 is said to be too insular and conceived in isolation from its south-east regional and sub-regional context. Undoubtedly this insularity represents a substantial concession by the G.L.C. to the sectional interests of its constituent borough councils. They have planning powers, granted under the London Government Act of 1963, which they jealously guard to serve their own interests in stabilizing declining borough populations and attracting offices, hotels, and industry, and taxable middle-class property. Current trends in government thinking, however, support opposing principles. Advisory reports have stressed the necessity for inter-borough planning to site shopping, school, and leisure centres in areas of greatest need, and a broad strategy to decentralize and disperse jobs and industry from the congested city centre. Furthermore, *The Strategic Plan for the South East Region*, sponsored by the government, emphasized the need to reach regional objectives through a revised and co-ordinated London metropolitan policy. Clearly, it will be quite some time before the differing agencies responsible for local, city, regional, and national strategic planning sort out their tangled and often hostile relationships.

In 1969 New York City's Planning Commission produced a six-volume city plan covering a number of critical policy issues and problems. These have to do with land uses, economic location and employment, schools and the pattern of education, demographic trends, housing needs, transport and highways, social life and recreational amenities, and personal mobility and new settlements. But there is little reference in the plans to the regional context of New York City's problems. This shortcoming may be partially explained by the fact that there is no official planning agency on the regional level. Nevertheless, the plan and the proposed solutions show no evidence of consultation with the Regional Plan Association, a prestigious voluntary body supported by public-spirited citizens and financed by the Russell Sage Foundation.

Chicago's Department of Development and Planning issued a new comprehensive plan for the city in 1966 'to enlarge human opportunities, to improve the environment, and to strengthen and diversify the economy'. It involves the construction of sixteen development areas containing in each one 150,000–250,000 persons with schools, shopping centres, parks, recreational facilities, and city services. Highway and transport will be improved, and a further 1,200 acres of Lake Michigan will be reclaimed for recreational purposes. But little real progress has been made, especially in co-ordinating efforts with the metropolitan area planning activities of the North-Eastern Illinois Planning Commission.

Metropolitan–regional planning runs into particular difficulty in America because of the intense feelings of hostility and fear which the people of suburbs and surrounding counties have of metropolitan domination. They see all attempts at consolidation with the city as 'big-city imperialism'. Each suburb seeks to maintain its own identity, and the politicians who represent them are hostile to any attempts at 'colonization'. Deep and persistent political conflicts divide the population of most metropolitan areas – for example, conflicts over taxes, the balance of authority, and housing and industrial location policies. There is also a fundamental social division between the city and the suburban ring which often takes the form of a conflict between lower classes and middle classes. When city–county amalgamation schemes are introduced, complex problems arise in organizing the relations among all the units. City–county amalgamation has not proven to be a very satisfactory method of rationalizing and harmonizing intercommunal administration and planning, mainly because too many small, disparate units are involved. The New York metropolitan region extends over twenty-two counties; Los Angeles over five. The Chicago metropolitan area extends even beyond the State of Illinois into Indiana, and Cook County, of which Chicago is a part, has 486 governmental units of various kinds. In San Francisco, city–county consolidation has done little to lessen the acute hostility towards overall planning and administration embracing the entire Bay Area.

Reforming Government Structures

Government structures in the great cities of the world define the relative degrees of power which can be wielded over the political, and hence the economic, resource delivery system that determines who gets what, where, when, and how. They also have certain characteristic defects that inhibit planning and implementing solutions to the urban crisis. Serious problems of governance, administration, and finance require immediate attention: outmoded functions and powers; inefficient and inadequate public services, caused largely by conflicts of interests, defective organization, and corruption; and restricted tax bases and financial bankruptcy.

At the most fundamental level – that of citizen involvement in government – all the evidence indicates a gross lack of direct popular control over an increasingly remote power elite and a complex baffling decision-making apparatus. Citizens have little power over or access to the executives, councillors, and public servants – the hallmarks of democracy – who determine how resources get allocated and to whom. Some big cities, like Buenos Aires, Mexico City, and New Delhi, have no representative local government. Many cities, such as Amsterdam, New York, Los Angeles, and Montreal, have less than fifty-five councillors representing their multi-million populations. In London, where much of the work of the Greater London Council takes place in a large number of small committees, it is almost impossible for ordinary citizens to trace the pattern of decision-making on crucial issues. City government in New York is a delicate balance of conflicting demands by dominant ethnic, religious, racial, and propertied interests – with little concern for the claims of unorganized minorities. And in Chicago, no one has as much power over city affairs as Mayor Daley, the head of municipal administration, presiding officer of the council, and boss of the powerful Cook County Democratic National Committee.

There is also cause for concern about the drastic reduction in popular representation that follows upon expansion of metropolitan control. Paris provides an example of this disturbing trend. The Ville de Paris has one councillor per 30,000 citizens, whereas in the communes of neighbouring departments it is less than one to 1,000 persons, much closer to the scale of small community living. When outlying communes are amalgamated a decrease has taken place in the ratio of councillors to citizens, thereby reducing the number of citizens taking part in local government.

Key metropolitan centres of power and wealth are subject to special forms of administration and controls which hinder the full expression of citizens' needs. National capitals like Washington, D.C., Buenos Aires, Mexico City, and New Delhi are 'special districts' under the control of national legislatures. New York City and London have 'special constitutions'. Tokyo has a unique elected Metropolitan Governor. In Paris, extraordinary powers are held by the government-appointed Prefect. The elected council is weak. It cannot debate many issues which concern citizens, and is strictly limited to those enumerated by law. The Prefect has wide powers over all municipal officials, the major social services, and the preparation of the draft budget and expenditures. He is the official representative of the city of Paris, and can suspend meetings of the council. Thus Paris cannot be considered in any real sense self-governing.

Attempts at comprehensive social planning get bypassed – or worse, mauled beyond recognition – in the hurly-burly of metropolitan politics. Planning proposals involving changes in the scope of administrative power or levels of taxation, for example, are treated from partisan political viewpoints. On issues like the extension of social services, labour and social democratic parties tend to urge generosity and the conservatives call for restraint, with a free hand given to private enterprise. Parties representing upper-middle-class persons and the car-owning public may endorse heavy expenditures on motorways; while others supporting the working class may favour improved public transport facilities, slum clearance, and nursery schools. The corruption and compromises which result preserve the system of power relations, while ensuring that whatever is done can be undone at the next election.

Cities are dependent on land and property taxes for income; but these cannot be easily increased to meet rising costs of land and the provision of services. The result is a proliferation of special taxes to attack city bankruptcy. Chicago taxes entertainment, dogs, fire insurance, and motor vehicles. Los Angeles gets nearly 16 per cent of its revenue from sales taxes. Rome collects taxes on rent receipts, building sites, domestic servants, billiard tables, and coffee-making machines. Even these special taxes are not enough, and many ailing cities now rely heavily on central and provincial finances to support municipal services like schools, roads, welfare, and housing. If this trend continues, cities may become totally dependent on government finances in the form of grants-in-aid, tax-sharing schemes on items like petrol, income, excess profits and capital gains, and equalization schemes by which government and wealthier localities contribute to the income of poorer districts.

Most great cities of the world exhibit a proliferation of *ad hoc* single-function authorities, e.g. school boards, port authorities, and gas, electricity, and pollution boards. There are at least two causes for this tendency. One is that the need is felt for specialist services which can be performed without the delay and conflicts of going through the democratic process. The other is that single-function authorities allow greater freedom to raise money in situations where there are existing legal limits on the fiscal powers of city governments. The Japanese have made extremely good use of this method, and Tokyo has a number of public corporations dealing with rapid transit, housing, expressway construction, urban renewal, and new town development. The proliferation of *ad hoc* bodies has serious drawbacks, however. Individually they cannot encompass or resolve city-wide problems and there is at present no adequate method of coordinating their work. Furthermore when several authorities are amalgamated into huge complexes, they do not satisfy the basic criterion of local democracy – representative election and public accountability. The Massachusetts Metropolitan District Commission is a case in point. It has responsibility for sewers, water supply, parks, and planning in Greater Boston but is in no sense an organ of local government because its members are appointed by and responsible to the Governor of the State.

Current research in all the world's capitals has pinpointed the necessity to reform obsolete governmental structures and functions; to raise new financial resources; and to upgrade municipal services. The United Nations report *Planning of Metropolitan Areas and New Towns* highlights these points with studies from Stockholm, Delhi, Prague, Tokyo, and the Randstad. So does the work of teams of planners reported by Simon R. Miles in *Metropolitan Problems: A Search for Comprehensive Solutions*. City managers in all spheres of activity need much more education to do their jobs. Job specifications need to be rewritten to allow for greater creativity and freedom for affecting change, and greater incentives to attract and hold the best talent. Once better qualified city managers and planners get on the job, say the authors of *Great Cities of the World*, a monumental survey of metropolitan government by Professor William A. Robson and Dr D. E. Regan of the London School of Economics, the inchoate metropolis will be tamed and 'we shall gradually create an ordered, coherent, decentralized metropolitan region'.

Planning Urban Futures

But we should not be seduced by these pithy phrases. Professional planners, designers, maintainers, and controllers of the built environment are part of the urban crisis. They must take partial responsibility along with politicians and administrators for the colossal lack of democratic intervention and management that exists. And they do not appear to be getting any closer to meeting the needs of the ordinary citizen as they carelessly play with futurist city-design schemes and techno-scientific methods to forecast urban futures.

Many architects, engineers, inventors, and entrepreneurs have proposed instant salvation for urban man if only he would try something new and different. Why not live, work, and play in the mega-structures of the Japanese architect Kenzo Tange and his New City over Tokyo Bay, the Sky City of the engineer Willem Frischman, with 300,000 people in a single building two miles high, or in the Russian Pchelnikov's Arctic City enclosed in a temperature-controlled dome of concrete and steel trusses?

American architects have proposed an Experimental Prototype Community of Tomorrow embodying new principles of city design and robot-ized computerized household and community living. There are even proposals for a McLuhanesque Global City, complete with a protective air curtain, and a closed-circuit, waste-recycling, power-producing, food-providing black box.

Buckminster Fuller, one of the most prolific inventors of urban futures, remembers that as a young man he was obsessed with the notion that a solution could be found to city problems by the creation of human settlements in totally new and sublime conditions. He was motivated by a desire to discover

how to develop environment-controlling devices for man that made it possible to exist under conditions that he had not been able to tolerate before – colder, warmer, wetter, drier – under conditions more favour-able to all his requirements, always giving him more and more time on his own, reducing his restraints and implementing his elective articulations, communications, travel, and acquisition of information.

From 1927 to the present Fuller produced some of the most far-reaching innovative proposals for controlled urban living ever imagined. For Manhattan he proposed his famous two-mile-in-diameter environment-controlled dome covering the midtown area. The waterways of Tokyo, Baltimore, and Toronto served as models for Fuller's conception of Floating Cities. One of these, called Tetrahedral City, was commissioned by an American housing and urban development agency. Three triangular walls, each containing thousands of living units, together with the base form a tetrahedron shape and the bottom of the superstructure contains a large park sunlit through special board openings on every fiftieth floor. Fuller claims that his Tetrahedral City can house a million people and all the machinery necessary for its operation, plus accommodation for seagoing vessels and jet planes. It could be moored offshore and linked with the mainland, or floated out into the ocean to serve as a permanent waterborne connecting link with new sources of international trade, passenger traffic, and marine exploration.

Designing new conditions for urban life is for many professionals an aesthetically rewarding and potentially useful way of brain-storming about urban futures. A generation of new architects following in the footsteps of Buckminster Fuller are filling the pages of architectural and ecological magazines with schemes for sky-floating geodesic-domed cities, air-deliverable skyscrapers, submarine islands, and rentable, autonomous-living black boxes within which man can move around the earth without hindrance. Schemes like these are part of a long history of visions of an ideal city; visions that are as old as the earliest soothsayers and the holy books of ancient religions. Vitruvius, a Roman architect at the time of Emperor Augustus, wondered about the form of the ideal city and wrote *De Architectura*, a book that influenced the Italian Renaissance. Sir Thomas More in 1516 gave it a name, Utopia – an imaginary, remote ideal place. Between the vision and the substance of the ideal city, however, lies the shadow of feasibility. Can it be built? What are the constraints of politics and custom? Where will the money come from? Who wants to live in it? And is it the only alternative for a viable, living urban future? Based largely on technological and physical innovations, these futuristic design answers to the urban crisis have several crucial limitations. They assume the unlimited adaptability of man's social nature and personality structure – which are already showing acute signs of stress and strain. And they do not really help us solve terrestrial problems of population location, productive activities, human relations, and environmental harmony. They would only transport these grave, deep-rooted problems elsewhere.

The emphasis of futurism in urban design is paralleled by the growth of a massive corps of highly trained technicians and scientists whose job is to organize and manage social and spatial systems for the benefit of their employers: government, industry, and other large corporate enterprises. The current tendency in planning is forecasting – peering into the future to identify the probable consequences of planning actions and to choose the most desirable results. Public sector investments are scanned by 'cost benefit analysts'. Computerized organization and management procedures are used to rationalize expenditures on social services with strategic political objectives. And more and more metropolitan authorities install the Programme–Planning–Budgeting System, a form of comprehensive cost accounting. Mathematical and statistical techniques are borrowed from natural sciences, operational research, management studies, and econometrics. And planners are busily engaged in using them on transport information, marketing data, and voting behaviour to forecast the ways in which individuals will attempt to fulfil their aspirations.

The study of urban futures is now a vital and profitable part of the new quarternary sector of man's productive activities – the knowledge industry based on the development and harvesting of world scientific information, its analysis and distribution to policy-makers. The futurist establishment is growing rapidly. Every big city has its futurist journals and centres, university courses in forecasting, and utopia factories and think-tanks. Another booming business is the manufacture of gaming simulation models, which like the games of 'Monopoly' and 'War' require players to highlight the acquisitive and destructive aspects of their personalities. The games simulate the conditions of the marketplace, for example, and are 'played' seriously by planners, property developers, corporation lawyers, and city managers – and billions of real currency and acres of prime sites are at stake. 'Brain-storming', once the pastime of fools and wise men, is now a major growth area. Teams of experts with differing backgrounds of expertise are organized: e.g. bio-chemists, atomic physicists, ecologists, electronics and data information specialists, transport engineers, aestheticians, sociologists, and landscape architects. They are asked to 'invent the future' by setting down a list of 'likely events' or by forecasting areas of future value conflicts in attitudes about income distribution, economic and population growth; family and marriage; learning, work, and leisure; and space and mobility. The results are processed and redistributed for further testing and validation; in the process, a pool of knowledge is created that can be readily tapped when necessary and applied to a specific problem for solution.

This emphasis on futurism and forecasting in urban planning has met with vociferous criticism. At the centre of the problem is the future of planning itself: how to manage the process of change in cities – to socialize the human services and enlarge the scope for individual and small-group decision and action – and thereby achieve the objective of increasing the welfare of all those who live and work in the city. Despite the increased mastery of technology, statistics, and science, and the vast storehouses of knowledge that exist, very little progress has been made in the implementation of social objectives in the great metropolises. Much of the work being done in high-powered think-tanks has to do with anticipating, evaluating, and acting to prevent disturbances in the social, political, and economic system. It is a kind of futuristic sociological espionage in which the data gathered and the 'solutions' are used against the people and communities who are most in need of help, and for those with the greatest power. There is no doubt that planning can be conducted 'scientifically' but the choices among future alternatives and, more importantly, whom to benefit by these choices, are political decisions from which the large mass of city dwellers are effectively barred from participation.

People and Planning

Demonstrations of discontent about their urban future by disgruntled city dwellers have forced some changes in planning structures. New devices of public involvement have been created, e.g. citizen participation strategies, public access to computer information terminals, freedom of information laws, and 'advocate planners' who work on behalf of community groups.

American planners, in particular, have gained experience in community planning through government-sponsored antipoverty programmes. Their role has been largely concerned with the amelioration of tensions between communities and City Hall. That is, their job is to increase the relevance of plans to community influentials, minority groups, or hard-to-convince non-participants, to minimize the adverse results of changes, and to instil a greater sense of pride and participation in the community's future life. Changes in the professional's 'definition of self' are also taking place in some universities where there is a recognition that new forms of planning education are needed to help beleaguered communities. Professor Melvin W. Webber of the University of California is one among a growing number of teachers who call for a better understanding of community social structures and political processes. He stresses the need for planning education which gives attention to consensus-building, coalition formation, persuasion, and bargaining between conflicting interest groups. Successful planning, according to this view, will assist in the identification of power-holders who can become political resource-suppliers, and allies on behalf of alternative goals and programmes.

In recent years in Britain much energy has been put into creating new modes of citizen participation in planning and renewal affairs. For example, the Town and Country Planning Act of

1968 provides citizens with a statutory right of access to information affecting them and an opportunity to make their views known to the local planning authority – and the authority must consider them. The 1969 Skeffington Committee report, *People and Planning*, took a broader view of these issues. It sees citizen participation as but one facet of changes taking place in local government:

It may be that the evolution of the structures of representative government which has concerned western nations for the last century and a half is now entering into a new phase. There is a growing demand by many groups for more opportunity to contribute, and for more say in the working out of policies which affect the people, not merely at election time, but continuously as proposals are being hammered out, and certainly as they are being implemented.

Nevertheless, the report concludes, there is little show from past efforts and in fact the public has made very little impact on the contents of plans. Many authorities have been more successful in informing people than in involving them, and those authorities who have made the most intensive efforts to publicize their efforts have done so when their proposals were all cut and dried. Urban Britain certainly needs a new form of local representative democracy; one which will give neighbourhoods and communities a firm participatory voice in city planning and administration. And communities in peril need free planning-aid services and advice to help them in their struggle against the worst abuses of planning agencies. 'It is a curious and discreditable anomaly of British Justice', as the Liverpool city planner F. J. C. Amos said in his presidential address at the Royal Town Planning Institute in 1971, 'that a man can obtain free legal aid to defend himself in a court of law, yet a community or group threatened with extinction or disaster can get no assistance for its defence.'

In all the major world cities urban democracy is threatened by two forces. One is the increasing dependence of politicians on esoteric knowledge and the new technocrats of institutional survival. The other is the decreasing ability of citizens to get the knowledge they need to participate in the decision-making process. The future will probably see a growth of more technocratic cadres. More sophisticated economic and statistical theories will be used as long-range planning aids. The accumulated knowledge will form the basis of city management and will also be central to attaining and maintaining political and bureaucratic power. Planners and city managers will tend to prevent their long-range plans from being upset. This will mean giving partisan interpretations to the public about the purposes and prospects of planning goals and their implementation. Given the complexity of both the planning process and the urban situation, the citizen will probably be unable to find out the implications of pursuing one plan, rather than another. His only options then will be disruption, protest, political withdrawal, or dependent ritual participation.

The problems which engulf us, the technocratic ways in which solutions are sought, and the decline of urban democracy all reveal a virulent anti-democratic tendency in operation. It may evidence the formation of a new oppressive urban society – one in which decision-makers dominate an increasingly large and alienated class of dependent participants in a programmed technocratic state. In the technocratic state, as Theodore Roszak, a social analyst, asserts in his book *The Making of a Counter-Culture*, 'those who govern justify themselves by appeal to technical experts who, in turn, justify themselves by appeal to scientific forms of knowledge. And beyond the authority of science, there is no appeal.' The technocratic society is a social form through which an industrial society reaches the peak of its organizational integration. Furthermore,

It is the ideal men usually have in mind when they speak of modernizing, updating, rationalizing, planning. Drawing upon such unquestionable imperatives as the demand for efficiency, for social security, for large-scale co-ordination of men and resources, for ever higher levels of affluence and ever more impressive manifestations of collective human power, the technocracy works to knit together the anachronistic gaps and fissures of the industrial society.

In the new technocratic society, where the scale of all human activities goes beyond the competence or comprehension of ordinary citizens, a new corps of trained experts develops. Then, says Roszak,

around this central core of experts who deal with large-scale public necessities, there grows up a circle of subsidiary experts who, battening on the general prestige of technical skill in the technocracy, assume authoritative influence over even the most seemingly personal aspects of life: sexual behaviour, child rearing, mental health, recreation, etc. In the technocracy everything aspires to become purely technical, the subject of professional attention. The technocracy is therefore the regime of experts – or those who employ the experts. Among its key institutions we find the 'think-tank', in which is housed a multi-billion dollar brainstorming industry that seeks to anticipate and integrate into the social planning quite simply everything on the scene. Thus, even before the general public has become fully aware of new developments, the technocracy has doped them out and laid its plans for adopting or rejecting, promoting or disparaging.

Traditional social and class divisions will be obscured or suppressed in the new society and the domination of technically competent elites will be widely accepted. Social conflicts will be different from those formed in the mechanized cities of 150 years ago around the principle of labour and socialist opposition to capitalism. The coming conflicts will be between those who control the institutions of information, mobility, and economic and political decision-making and those who have been reduced to a base condition of dependent participation. A condition of subordination in which a man's relationship to the social structure of society and its rewards is one accorded to him by the ruling class in a way compatible with the maintenance of its domination. A condition in which the potency of non-terroristic seduction, manipulation, and induced conformism far exceeds that of abject misery, the whiplash of chronic poverty and malnutrition, or the butt of a policeman's club.

Planning geared to the ends of the technocratic society is basically undemocratic. Planners are too remote, and too ignorant of urban social reality. They are incapable of developing sensitive indicators of popular feeling, of opening up access to the resource-distribution system, or of really questioning the side effects, long-term impact, and social costs of planning decisions. It would be entirely useless to try and appeal to the majority of engineers, for example, to change their ways and become 'conscientious objectors', says Dennis Gabor, a professor at the Imperial College of Technology, London, in his book *Inventing the Future*. 'Most of them do not have, and do not want to have, an integrated view of the economic and social world. They feel quite happy in this ignorance which relieves them of responsibility. The initiative must come not from them but from society.'

Nothing short of a social revolution will be necessary to change the course of future urban history and to counteract the technocratic society. Why? Because there is one underlying fact that stands out clearly in our discussion of the urban crisis. Neither the urban explosion, central area decay and suburban sprawl, congestion, pollution, nor any of the urban social problems I have dealt with can find its causes or its cures in the city. Their origins are not local, or any longer territorially defined. These are societal problems, observable on a national and international scale, that are localized in cities. They are not peculiar to cities or susceptible to correction by cities or city dwellers acting on their own.

The ills of the urban crisis are, in fact, all interconnected with our life-styles, work habits, activities, and forms of social organization and settlement. They reveal permanent flaws in modern urban society. They are extensions of historical, political, and economic motives which only now, as the disruptive technological expressions of these flaws become more visible, we have begun to question. There is no doubt that the tensions existing between the structures of government and planning and unmet human needs can be resolved. We do not lack experts, if these are what is needed. The fact is that there are too many experts tinkering with too many short-term and parochial problems. What will be required is that changes take place at all levels in our lives. On the local level there must be renewed positive action for democratic popular control and management of urban affairs. People must decide to stop revolving around technocratic authoritarian centres and seek new political and cultural directions. A new movement for a responsible technology must be created which unites many diverse sections of the public and professions, and moves planning towards the liberation of individuals and communities.

Present efforts must be continued to accommodate urban populations, to integrate technology into complex environments, to plan industrialization and urbanization, and to properly manage land and resources. But it will not be enough merely to get technology to eradicate and patch up damage – or to be more considerate in the future. It will not be enough to inject new understanding into old value systems based on maximized productivity and competition. Competition must be phased out and replaced by new socially responsible economies, political forms, and social values. We cannot retreat from our dilemmas, but we can seek improved methods of co-ordinating our fragmented thought and action about cities, technology and the environment.

Without them, high-level-technology urban societies will produce either chaos or tyranny, or both. Since we will not retreat to older forms of unity, we have to seek it at a new level by such drastic innovations as restructuring the market and productive relations, government, politics, and school systems, and our basic cultural beliefs and values.

Bibliography

In writing this book I have drawn upon a growing body of opinion and academic literature devoted to urban planning and environmental affairs. My indebtedness is indicated in the bibliography which consists mainly of cited sources and a selection of relevant books and reports. Acknowledgements are also due to Nick Holliman and Andrew McKillop for their research assistance.

ALDOUS, TONY, *Battle for the Environment* (London: Fontana, 1972).
L'Architecture d'Aujourd'hui (January 1970).
ARENDT, HANNAH, *On Violence* (London: Allen Lane, 1970; New York: Harcourt Brace Jovanovich).
ASH, MAURICE, *A Guide to the Structure of London* (Bath: Adams & Dart, 1972).
ASH, MAURICE, *Regions of Tomorrow: Towards the Open City* (London: Adams & Mackay, 1969; New York: Schocken Books).

BANFIELD, EDWARD C. (ed.), *Urban Government* (New York: The Free Press, 2nd edn, 1969).
BELL, GWEN and TYRWHITT, JACQUELINE (eds.), *Human Identity in the Urban Environment* (London: Penguin, 1972).
BRECKENFIELD, GURNEY, *Columbia and the New Cities* (New York: Ives Washburn, 1971).
BREESE, GERALD, *Urbanization in Newly Developing Countries* (Englewood Cliffs, N.J.: Prentice-Hall, 1966).
BUCHANAN, COLIN, *Traffic in Towns:* Reports of the Steering Group and Working Group led by Colin Buchanan (London: Penguin, 1964).
BURNEY, ELIZABETH, *Housing on Trial* (London: Oxford University Press, 1967).

CALDER, NIGEL, *Technopolis: Social Control of the Uses of Science* (London: Panther Books, 1970; New York: Simon & Schuster).
CARSON, RACHEL, *Silent Spring* (London: Penguin Books; New York: Houghton Mifflin, 1962).
Cities (London: A 'Scientific American' Book by Pelican, 1965).

COHN-BENDIT, DANIEL and GABRIEL, *Obsolete Communism: The Left-Wing Alternative* (London: Penguin, 1969; New York: McGraw-Hill).

COLES, ROBERT, 'Life Like It Is in the Alley', in *Daedalus*, 'The Conscience of the City' (Fall 1968).

COMMONER, BARRY, *Science and Survival* (London: Gollancz, 1966; New York: Ballantine Books).

The Comprehensive Plan of Chicago (Chicago Department of Development and Planning, 1966).

COTTRELL, FRED, *Energy and Society* (New York: McGraw-Hill, 1955).

Daedalus, Journal of the American Academy of Arts & Sciences, 'The Conscience of the City' (Fall 1968).

DE BELL, GARRETT (ed.), *The Environmental Handbook* (New York: A Ballantine/Friends of the Earth Book, 1970).

DICKINSON, ROBERT E., *City and Region: A Geographical Interpretation* (London: Routledge & Kegan Paul, Fifth Impression 1964; New York: Humanities Press).

DICKINSON, ROBERT E., *The West European City* (London: Routledge & Kegan Paul, 2nd edn, 1961; New York: Humanities Press).

DORE, RONALD P., *City Life in Japan* (U.S.A.: University of California Press, 1958).

DOXIADIS, CONSTANTINOS, *Ekistics: An Introduction to the Science of Human Settlements* (London: Oxford University Press, 1960).

DOXIADIS, CONSTANTINOS, *Emergence and Growth of an Urban Region* (U.S.A.: Detroit Edison Company, 1970).

DURKHEIM, EMILE, *Suicide: A Study in Sociology*, translated by George Simpson (New York: Free Press, 1951); *see also* chapter on social structure and anomie in Robert K. Merton – *Social Theory and Social Structure*, revised edition (New York: Free Press, 1957).

The Ecologist: Blueprint for Survival (January 1972).

EHRLICH, PAUL R. and ANNE H., *Population, Resources, Environment* (U.S.A.: W. H. Freeman, 1970).

ENGELS, FRIEDRICH, *The Condition of the Working Class in England* (London: Panther Books, 1969; U.S.A.: Stanford University Press).

ERIKSON, ERIK, *Identity: Youth and Crisis* (London: Faber & Faber, 1968; New York: W. W. Norton & Company).

'La gauche américaine et la question de l'écologie', *Espaces et Sociétés*, revue critique internationale de l'aménagement de l'architecture et de l'urbanisation, Décembre 1971, no. 4, Henri Lefebvre et Anatole Kopp, directeurs.

FORRESTER, JAY W., *Urban Dynamics* (Cambridge, Mass.: M.I.T. Press, 1969).

FORRESTER, JAY W., *World Dynamics* (U.S.A.: Wright-Allen Press, 1971).

Fortune Magazine, special issue on the environment (February 1970).

Fortune Magazine, special issue on transportation (July 1971).

FREEDMAN, RONALD, (ed.), *Population: The Vital Revolution* (New York: Doubleday, 1964).

FROMM, ERICH, *Escape from Freedom* (New York: Rinehart, 1941).

FULLER, R. BUCKMINSTER, *Comprehensive Design Strategy, World Resources Inventory Phase II* (U.S.A.: University of Illinois, 1967).

GABOR, DENNIS, *Inventing the Future* (London: Pelican, 1964; New York: Alfred A. Knopf).

GALBRAITH, JOHN, *The New Industrial State* (New York: Houghton Mifflin, 1969).

GANS, HERBERT J., *The Levittowners* (London: Allen Lane the Penguin Press, 1967; New York: Random House).

GEDDES, PATRICK, *Cities in Evolution* (London: Williams & Norgate, 1949; New York: Harper & Row).

GLAZER, NATHAN and MOYNIHAN, DANIEL P., *Beyond the Melting Pot* (Cambridge, Mass.: M.I.T. Press, 2nd edn, 1970).

GOODMAN, ROBERT, *After the Planners* (London: Pelican, 1972; New York: Simon & Schuster).

GOTTMANN, JEAN, *Megalopolis: The Urbanized Northeastern Seaboard of the United States* (Cambridge, Mass.: M.I.T. Press, 1961).

Greater London Council Development Plan Report of Studies (London: G.L.C., 1969).

GRUEN, VICTOR, *The Heart of Our Cities* (London: Thames & Hudson, 1965; New York: Simon & Schuster).

GUTKIND, ERWIN, *Urban Development in Southern Europe: Italy and Greece* (New York: Free Press of Glencoe, 1969).

HALL, PETER, *London 2000* (London: Faber & Faber, 1971; New York: Praeger).

HALL, PETER, *World Cities* (London: Weidenfeld & Nicolson, 1966; New York: McGraw-Hill).

HOLLAND, LAURENCE B. (ed.), *Who Designs America?* (New York: Doubleday, 1966).

HORNEY, KAREN, *The Neurotic Personality of Our Time* (New York: Norton, 1937; London: Routledge & Kegan Paul).

HOWARD, EBENEZER, *Garden Cities of Tomorrow* (London: Faber & Faber, 1945; Cambridge, Mass.: M.I.T. Press).

HUNTER, DAVID R., *The Slums: Challenge and Response* (New York: Free Press, 1968).

JACOBS, JANE, *The Economy of Cities* (London: Jonathan Cape, 1969; New York: Random House).

169

KOPP, ANATOLE, *Town and Revolution* (London: Thames & Hudson, 1970; New York: Braziller).

LAING, R. D. and COOPER, DAVID G., *Dialectics of Liberation* (London: Penguin, 1969).

LEARY, TIMOTHY, *The Politics of Ecstasy* (London: Paladin, 1970; New York: G. P. Putnam's Sons, 1968).

LEFEBVRE, HENRI, *La pensée marxiste et la ville* (Paris: Casterman poche, 1972).

LEFEBVRE, HENRI, *La révolution urbaine* (Paris: Gallimard, 1970).

LIPSET, SEYMOUR and SCHAFTLANDER, GERALD, *They Would Rather Be Left* (Boston: Little, Brown, 1971).

Man's Impact on the Global Environment: Report of the Study of Critical Environmental Problems (Cambridge: M.I.T. Press, 1970).

MEADOWS, PAUL and MIZRUCHI, E. H., *Urbanism, Urbanization, and Change* (U.S.A.: Addison-Wesley Publishing Co., 1969).

MERTON, ROBERT K. and NISBET, ROBERT, *Contemporary Social Problems* (New York: Harcourt Brace Jovanovich, 3rd edn, 1971).

MILES, SIMON R. (ed.), *Metropolitan Problems: A Search for Comprehensive Solutions* (Toronto: Methuen, 1970).

MILLS, C. WRIGHT, *White Collar* (New York: Oxford University Press, 1956).

MUMFORD, LEWIS, *The City in History* (London: Secker & Warburg, 1961; New York: Harcourt Brace Jovanovich).

MUMFORD, LEWIS, *The Highway and the City* (London: Secker & Warburg, 1964).

NAKANE, CHIE, Japanese Society (London: Weidenfeld & Nicolson, 1970; U.S.A.: University of California Press).

National Advisory Commission on Civil Disorders, *Report* (New York: Bantam Books, 1968).

New York City Planning Commission: *The Plan for New York City* (Cambridge, Mass.: M.I.T. Press, 1969).

ODUM, HOWARD T., *Environment, Power and Society* (New York: Wiley, 1971).

OPPENHEIMER, MARTIN, *Urban Guerrilla* (London: Penguin, 1970; New York: Quadrangle, 1969).

P.A.D.O.G.: Plan d'Aménagement et d'Organisation Générale de la Région Parisienne; Avant-Projet de Programme Duodécennal pour la Région de Paris (District de la Région de Paris, Imprimerie Municipale, Paris 1963). (*See also Schema Directeur d'Aménagement et d'Urbanisme de la Région Parisienne*, District de la Région de Paris, 1965).

PARKINS, MAURICE F., *City Planning in Soviet Russia: With an Interpretative Bibliography* (U.S.A.: University of Chicago Press, 1953).

PERIN, CONSTANCE, *With Man In Mind* (Cambridge, Mass.: M.I.T. Press, 1970).

RAO, V. K. R. V. and DESAI, P. B., *Greater Delhi: A Study in Urbanisation 1940-57* (Bombay: Asia Publishing House, 1965).

REICH, CHARLES A., *The Greening of America* (New York: Random House, 1970; London: Penguin).

ROACH, JACK L. and JANET K. (eds.), *Poverty: Selected Readings* (London: Penguin, 1972).

ROBSON, WILLIAM A. and REGAN, D. E., *Great Cities of the World* (London: George Allen & Unwin, 3rd edn, 1972, 2 volumes).

ROSZAK, THEODORE, *The Making of a Counter-Culture: Reflections on the Technocratic Society and its Youthful Opposition* (London: Faber & Faber, 1970; New York: Doubleday).

SAMPSON, ANTHONY, *The New Europeans* (London: Panther Books, 1971).

SENNETT, RICHARD, *The Uses of Disorder* (London: Allen Lane the Penguin Press, 1970; New York: Alfred A. Knopf).

SJOBERG, GIDEON, *The Preindustrial City* (New York: The Free Press, 1960).

SLATER, PHILIP E., *The Pursuit of Loneliness: American Culture at the Breaking Point* (London: Allen Lane the Penguin Press, 1970; Boston: Beacon Press).

SROLE, LEO et al., *Mental Health in the Metropolis* (New York: McGraw-Hill, 1962).

STEWART, MURRAY (ed.), *The City: Problems of Planning: Selected Readings* (London: Penguin, 1972).

SULLIVAN, HARRY STACK, *Conceptions of Modern Psychiatry* (New York: Norton, 1953).

TITMUSS, RICHARD, 'Poverty versus Inequality', in *Poverty*, edited by Jack L. Roach and Janet K. Roach (London: Penguin, 1972).

TOFFLER, ALVIN, *Future Shock* (London: Bodley Head, 1970; New York: Random House).

Tomorrow's London (London: Greater London Council, 1969).

TOURAINE, ALAIN, *The Post-Industrial Society* (New York: Random House, 1971).

TOYNBEE, ARNOLD, *Cities on the Move* (London: Oxford University Press, 1970).

Traffic Quarterly, Vol. XXIV, no. 2, April 1970.

United Nations in Co-operation with the United Auto Workers: *Symposium on the Impact of Urbanization on Man's Environment*, 13–20 June 1970, *Statement and Conclusions* (Washington, D.C.: United Auto Workers, Department of International Affairs, 1970).

United Nations Conference on the Human Environment: *Development and Environment* (Subject Area V) report by the Secretary General A/Conf. 48/10, 22 December 1971, English.

United Nations: *Planning of Metropolitan Areas and New Towns* (New York: United Nations, 1967).

United States Congress: *Basic Laws and Authorities on Housing and Urban Development 1970* (Washington, D.C.: Government Printing Office, 1970).

United States Department of Health, Education, and Welfare: *Environmental Health Problems* (Rockville, Maryland: U.S. Department of Health, Education, and Welfare, Public Health Service, Environmental Health Service, 1970).

United States Department of Housing and Urban Development: *Tomorrow's Transportation – New Systems for the Urban Future* (Washington, D.C.: U.S. Department of Housing and Urban Development, June 1968).

United States Government: *Violent Crime: A Task Force Report to the National Commission on the Causes and Prevention of Violence* (Washington, D.C.: U.S. Government Printing Office, 1970).

Urbanisation and Planning in France; joint publication: International Federation for Housing and Planning – Centre de Recherche d'Urbanisme (Paris 1968).

WALKER, DANIEL, Director of the Chicago Study Team, *Rights in Conflict*, a report submitted to the National Commission on the Causes and Prevention of Violence (New York: Bantam Books, 1968).

WALSH, ANNMARIE HAUCK, *The Urban Challenge to Government: An International Comparison of Thirteen Cities* (New York: Praeger, 1969).

WEAVER, ROBERT C., *The Urban Complex* (New York: Doubleday Anchor Books, 1964).

WILLMOTT, PETER and YOUNG, MICHAEL, *Family and Class in a London Suburb* (London: Mentor, 1967; New York: Humanities Press).

WILSON, JAMES Q. (ed.), *The Metropolitan Enigma* (Cambridge, Mass.: Harvard University Press, 1967, 1968).

WOLMAN, ABEL, 'The Metabolism of Cities' in *Scientific American*, September 1965, Vol. 213, no. 3.

Index

Abercrombie, Sir Patrick, 146
Abrams, Charles, 23
Accra, Tema new town, 145
Africa, population growth in cities, 24–5
Air pollution, 96–100, 101–6
Aircraft noise, 99
Alberts, Professor Gerd, 38
Aldous, Tony, 71
Alienation, 117, 120–1
Amendola, Gianfranco, 98
Amos, F. J. C., 162
Antwerp, 38, 39
Asia, urban populations of, 24
Athens, squatters of, 60–1

Bacon, Vinton W., 111
Battery Park City (Manhattan), 150
Belgium:
  motorways, 76
  slums and unmodernized dwellings,
    49
Berlin, political violence in, 136
Birth rate, 17
Black ghetto revolt, 130–4
Blocked opportunity, 124–30
Boston, transport problems of the poor,
  90
'Bos-Wash', the, 40–1, 64, 97
Brandt, Chancellor Willy, 125
Breese, Gerald, 25
Britain:
  housing inadequacies, 50
  immigrant workers, 124–5
  loss of identity, 118
  metropolitan–regional management,
    152
  motor vehicles, numbers, 70, 71
  new towns, 145–9
  planning of urban futures, 161–2
  road congestion, 69–73
  urban transport planning, 73–4
  see also England
British Airports Authority, 99
British Medical Research Council, 99
British Rail, 73
Brown, H. Rap, 133
Buchanan, Professor Colin, 69–70, 72,
  73–4, 92
Burney, Elizabeth, 125

Calcutta, poverty in, 51
Canada:
  political violence in, 136–7
  St Lawrence Seaway megalopolis, 43–4
Carmichael, Stokely, 131, 132
Carveyor, the, 144
Cedar-Riverside (Minneapolis), 150
Chaban-Delmas, M., 126
Chicago:
  black migrants, 129
  ethnic groups, 128–30

European immigrant families, 128–9
metropolitan–regional planning, 153,
  155
sludge disposal, 111
China, urban population, 25
Cities:
  changes in the seventeenth and eight-
    eenth centuries, 28–9
  in the nineteenth century, 29–30
  out of phase with ecological reality,
    114–15
  population growth in, 17–19, 23–5
  problems of life in, 117–19
  six 'false friends of the city', 93–4
  world's first, 26–8
  see also individual cities: London, Mos-
    cow, Paris, etc.
City in History, The, 52
Clean Air Act 1968 99
Coles, Robert, 123
Common Market, see European Econo-
  mic Community
Common Market and the Common Man,
  The, 20
Conde, Marie Martins, 126
Condition of the Working Class in Eng-
  land, 105
Conflict and violence, 117–40, 164
Consolidated Edison, 97
Containerization, 39
Copenhagen, suburbanization, 65
Crime in cities, 124
Cutler, Horace, 73

Daley, Mayor Richard, 130, 155
Davis, Professor Kingsley, 23
De Gaulle, Charles, 135
Delhi, population, 24
Detroit, urban area of, 42–3
Developing nations, poverty and poor
  housing, 51
Dialectics of disorder, 138–40
Domencich, Thomas, 90
Doxiadis, Dr Constantinos A., 43–4
Durkheim, Emile 120

Eckardt, Wolf Von, 41
Economic development and technological change, effects of, 19–20
Economic surpluses, early production
  of, 26
Ekistics (science of human settlements),
  43
Emergence and Growth of an Urban
  Region, 43
England:
  as the first urbanized and industrialized
    nation, 29
  urban population in the nineteenth
    century, 29
  see also Britain

Engels, Friedrich, 105
Environmental Action Groups, 109–10
Erikson, Erik, 139
Europe:
 air transport, 78
 anti-pollution projects and programmes, 112–14
 E-routes, 77
 Golden Triangle of, 38–40
 motorways of, 77
 rail transport, 77–8
 road-building programmes, 76–7
 traffic congestion problems, 76–8
European Economic Community:
 effects on city growth, 40
 foreign workers, 20, 21–2, 125, 127–8
 regions of, 22
 slums and unmodernized dwellings,
  48–50
European urbanization, 27–8
Experimental Prototype Community of
 Tomorrow, 158

Feltrinelli, 136
Floating Cities, 158
Folk societies, 26
Ford, Henry, 132
Forecasting, 159–60
France:
 new towns, 145
 poor dwellings, 49
 roads of, 76
Franklin Town (Philadelphia), 150
French Centre of Urban Research, 112
Frischman, Willem, 157
Fromm, Erich, 121
Front de Libération du Québec (F.L.Q.)
 136–7
Fuller, Buckminster, 158
Futurism, in urban design, 157–61

Gabor, Professor Dennis, 115, 164
Gans, Herbert, 57, 62, 64
Germany:
 autobahns, 76–7
 dwellings needing modernization or
  replacement, 49
 immigrant foreign workers, 125
Ghettos, see Black ghetto revolt
Gillot, Jacky, 109
Golden Triangle of Europe, 38–40
Gorki, Maxim, 34
Gottmann, Jean, 40, 41
Government structures and functions,
 need to reform, 154–7
Great Lakes Megalopolis, 42–3
Greater London Council, 154
 metropolitan–regional issues, 152
 road congestion, 70, 71
Greater London Development Plan, 62,
 152
Gruen, Victor, 93–4

Haar, Professor Charles, 151
Hall, Peter, 52, 56
Hamburg, 39
Hatcher, Richard, 132
Hauser, Philip, 15–16
Haussmann, Baron, 75
Heyerdahl, Thor, 107
Highway and the City, The, 66
Highways, impact of, 95
Holland:
 immigrant foreign workers, 125–6
 steel industry, 39
Holland, Laurence B., 93
'Homes Before Roads' campaign, 71
Hong Kong:

population growth, 24
squatters of, 60
Horney, Karen, 121
Housing:
 immigrant foreign workers, 126–7
 see also Slums
Housing and Development Act 1970
 (USA), 149–50
Housing on Trial, 125
Howard, Ebenezer, 146

Immigrant workers, problem of, 124–9
Immigration Act 1971, 128
Industry, British policy on location of, 39
Inequality and poverty, 121–4
Inventing the Future, 164
Italy:
 culture shock in, 118
 motor vehicles, 74–5
 poor dwellings, 49
 roads of, 77
 transport system, 74–5
 water pollution, 98
Izvestia, 103, 114

Jacobs, Jane, 151
Japan, 35 see also Tokyo
Japanese Psychological Association, 119
Jewish community of the USA, 128–9
John Birch Society, 137
Johnson, Alfred, 82

Ki Kimura, 35
King, Martin Luther, 130
Kock, M. Marc, 128
Kraft, Gerald, 90
Krokodil, 114
Kuala Lumpur, Petaling Jaya new town,
 145
Ku Klux Klan, 137

Lake Tahoe, water treatment facility,
 111
Latin America:
 political violence, 136
 urban population growth, 24
League for the Defence of the Rights of
 of Man, 128
Levitt & Sons, 55, 57, 149
London, 31–2
 air pollution, 99–100
 areas of, 31
 environmental problems, 109
 noise pollution, 98–9
 population in nineteenth century, 29
 position in Golden Triangle of Europe,
  38–9
 problems of life in, 118
 road congestion, 70–1
 suburbs of, 53–4, 65
 transport system, 73
 water pollution, 98
London Government Act 1963, 152
London Transport Executive, 73
Los Angeles:
 air pollution, 97–8
 anti-pollution measures, 110
 motorized city, 53, 65
Lower Depths, The, 34

Making of a Counter Culture, The, 163
McLuhanesque Global City, 158
Meadows, Dr Dennis L., 115
Megalopolis:
 advent of, 40–4
 'Bos-Wash', The, 40–1, 64, 97
 Great Lakes, 42–3
 St Lawrence Seaway, 43–4

Megalopolis: The Urbanized Northeasten Seaboard of the United States, 40-1
Metropolitan politics, 154-7
Metropolitan Problems: A Search for Comprehensive Solutions, 157
Metropolitan regions, growth of, 30-40
Mexico City:
  slums of, 46
  student protests, 135
Migration from rural to urban areas, 21-5, 29-30, 38
Milan, political violence, 136
Mills, C. Wright, 120
Milton Keynes new town, 147-8
Minobe, Ryokichi, 100-1
Minutemen, the, 137
Monteneros, the, 136
More, Sir Thomas, 159
Mortality rate, 17
Moscow, 33-4
  air pollution, 103-4
  areas of, 34
  housing problems, 62-4
  noise pollution, 103
  planning problems in, 34
  refuse disposal, 103
  slums of, 46
  suburbanization, 65
  Telovaia Elektrotsentral, 103-4
  transport system, 75
  water pollution, 104
Motor vehicles:
  dominance of, 70, 71, 74-6, 78-9, 84, 85, 92-3
  European producers of, 76
Motorized societies, 53, 65, 92-3
Mumford, Lewis, 52, 66, 94
Myers, Sumner, 89-90

Nader, Ralph, 90
National Association for the Advancement of Coloured People, 131
NATO, anti-pollution and economic development programmes, 112
Netherlands:
  motorways, 76
  poor dwellings, 49
New towns, 145-51
New York City:
  air pollution, 96-7
  air traffic congestion, 69
  city government, 154-5
  expressways, 69
  metropolitan-regional planning, 152-3, 154
  pollution from motor vehicles, 69
  road congestion, 69
  rural areas (exurbia), 56
  slums of, 86
  social problems in, 117-18
  suburbanization, 55-6
  subway system, 67-8
  transport authorities, 68-9
  transport problems, 67-9, 86-7
Noise pollution, 98-9, 103, 106
Northern Ireland, political violence, 136

Oishi, Boichi, 110
Oporto, slums of, 46
Organization for Economic Cooperation and Development, 112

Paris, 32-3
  areas of, 32-3
  city government 155
  immigrant workers, 126-7
  metropolitan-regional management, 152

slums of, 46
student protests, 134-5
suburbanization of, 54-5, 65
transport system, 75-6
Pchelnikov, 157
Peccei, Dr Aurelio, 98
Pedestrian precincts, 143-4
Perin, Constance, 138-9
Perloff, Harvey, 87-8
Personal Rapid Transport (PRT), 142-3
Philadelphia, Lindenwold suburban line, 68
Plan for New York City, The, 67
Planning of Metropolitan Areas and New Towns, 157
Police measures to repress violence, 137
Political violence, 136-7
Pollution:
  air pollution, 96-100, 101-6
  dealing with the problem of, 108-14
  fall-out, 107-8
  garbage disposal, 100-1, 103
  in Neolithic Age, 104-5
  in nineteenth century, 105
  noise pollution, 98 9, 103, 106
  water pollution, 98, 100, 104, 111
Pompidou, Georges, 135
Population:
  distribution and increase, 16
  fifteen countries with the largest, 18
  growth in, 15-17
  large cities, 17-19
  in twentieth century, 105-6
  see also under individual cities: London, Moscow etc.
Posokhin, Mikhail, 104
Poverty and inequality, 121-2
Power, Jonathan, 126
Preindustrial City, The, 23
Pre-industrial civilization, 27-8
Pursuit of Loneliness, The, 121

Racial Attitudes in Fifteen American Cities, 131
Racial problems, 124-34
Rail transport, innovations, 142
Randstad, The (Holland), 36-7, 65
Regan, Dr D. E., 157
Respiratory disease and pollution, 99
'Retail Revolution' in the USA, 74
Revelle, Richard, 108
Revolutionary Action Movement of New York, 137
Rhine-Ruhr, 37-8
  anti-pollution measures, 110-11
  constituent parts, 37-8
  transport system, 75
Road accidents, 92-3
Robson, Professor William A., 157
Rome:
  conservationist groups, 98
  water pollution, 98
Romney, George, 83
Rose, Professor Arnold, 126
Rossi, Professor Peter, 131
Roszak, Theodore, 163-4
Roth, Gabriel, 72-3
Rouse, James W., 149

St Lawrence Seaway megalopolis, 43-4
San Francisco, metropolitan-regional planning, 154
Santiago de Chile, *poblaciones* of, 59
Self, Professor Peter, 109
Sennett, Dr Richard, 138-9
Sjoberg, Gideon, 23
Skeffington Committee, 162
Slater, Philip, 121
Sludge disposal, 111

Slums:
definition of, 45–8
Europe, 48–50
growth of, 48–51
legislation and, 61–4
in suburbs, 58–61
Social welfare, 121–4
Solutions to urban problems, 141–66
Soviet Union:
pollution control, 113–14
urban population, 24
Squatters' settlements, 58–61
Srole, Professor Leo, 120
Stockholm, new towns, 145
Student protests, 134–5
Suburbanization, 51–8, 64–5
Suburbs, slums in, 58–61
Sullivan, Harry Stack, 121
Sweden, pollution, 108

Tange, Kenzo, 157
Taxation, 156
Technocratic society, 162–6
Technological change, 19–20
Telecanape, the, 144
Terrorist violence, 136–7
Tetrahedral City, 158
Third World, migration to newly developed areas of, 23
Thorne, Neil, 70
Titmuss, Professor Richard, 122–3
Tokyo, 34–6
air pollution, 101, 102–3
anti-pollution measures, 102
areas of, 36
Capital Region Development Commission, 151–2
city government, 155
culture shock, 118–19
environmental action groups, 109–10
fast growth of, 35–6
garbage disposal, 100–1
Hino new town, 145
legislation regarding pollution, 110
motor vehicles, 74
overcrowding in, 36
population, 35, 36
slums, 46
student protests, 135–6
transport system, 74
water pollution, 100
youth, stresses and strains on, 119
Toronto, Bramlea new town, 145
Town and Country Planning Act 1968
161–2
Town and Country Planning Association, 109
Traffic congestion problem, 94–5
Traffic in Towns, 69, 72, 92
Tramways, 142
Transport:
'auto-taxi service' 142
'guided busway', the, 142
monorails, 142
'never-stop' belt systems, 144
pedestrian conveyors, 144
Personal Rapid Transport, 142–3
problems of, 66–95
solution to problems, 141–5
world cities, systems reaching breaking point, 91–5
Trud, 114
Tupamaros, the, 136

United States of America:
air pollution, 96–8, 106
American Association of State Highway Officials, 82
bad housing and poverty, 50–1
black ghetto revolt, 130–4
'Bos-Wash', the, 40–1, 64, 97
bus transport, 84–5
costs of cleaning up waste, 108
expressways, 80, 84
'Energy Society' and pollution, 105–6
Great Lakes megalopolis, 42–3
Highway Act, 80
Holiday Motor Inns, 81
immigrant workers, 128–9
Interstate Highway controversy, 80–3
Jewish communities, 128–9
metropolitan–regional planning, 152–3
motor cars, 78–9, 84, 85
National Conference of Governors, 82
National Conference of Mayors, 82
new towns, 149–51
noise pollution, 106
public transport, 79–80, 84–91
road congestion, 78–80
slum clearance legislation, 61–2
suburbanization, 64–5
terrorist activities in cities, 137
transport:
Dial-a-Bus system, 88
Jitney buses, 88
problems of, 78–91
taxi-bus systems, 88–9
unemployment and transportation, link between, 87–8
urban population, 24
waste disposal, 106–7
water pollution, 107, 111
Urban democracy, decline of, 162–5
Urbanization in Newly Developing Countries, 25
Urbanized societies, world trend towards, 25–31
Uses of Disorder, The, 138
Uzbekistan Republic, slums of, 46

Violence-prone cities, 134–8
Vitruvius, 159
Volpe, John A., 83

Walker, Peter, 109
Waste disposal, 100–1, 103, 106–8, 113
Water pollution, 98, 100, 104, 107, 111
Weathermen, the, 137
Webber, Professor Melvin W., 161
Welfare Island (New York), 150
White Collar, 120
Who Designs America?, 93
Who Riots?, 131
Willmott, Peter, 53
With Man in Mind, 138
Women, social inequality, 123
Woodford (England), 53–4
Workers, migration from rural to urban areas, 20–3; see also Immigrant workers
World Cities, 52

Young, Michael, 53

Zangheri, Professor Renato, 75
Zengakuren, the, 136
Znaniecki, Florian, 129

Blair

DATE DUE

MAY 2			
MAR 3 1978			
APR 2 1 1984			